OSS

Stories that can now be told

by

Dorothy Ringlesbach

author**HOUSE**™

1663 LIBERTY DRIVE, SUITE 200
BLOOMINGTON, INDIANA 47403
(800) 839-8640
WWW.AUTHORHOUSE.COM

First published by AuthorHouse 03/09/05

ISBN: 1-4208-1582-2 (sc)
ISBN: 1-42081583-0 (dj)

Library of Congress Control Number: 2004099197

Printed in the United States of America
Bloomington, Indiana
This book is printed on acid-free paper.

Cover credit to L.M. Ledbetter Jr.

TABLE OF CONTENTS

INTRODUCTION

When Jack and I were married twenty-five years ago I knew nothing about the OSS (Office of Strategic Services) and in fact I had never heard about this branch of service. All he mentioned at that time was a little of the history of the group and a few funny things that happened to him and the crew he flew with.

This organization came about as a result of President Roosevelt's frustration with the squabbling between the Army and Naval intelligence in the State Department. He called on his good friend, William Donovan, to come to Washington and set up some kind of intelligence service. As a result this outfit became one of the best-kept secrets of WW II.

The OSS was composed of several "arms" with General Donovan in charge of the main one in Washington. The other vital arms consisted of the air arm, the Carpetbaggers, the Jedburgs or Joes and Josephine's as the women were known, and then there were also couriers who were either SOE or OSS who liased between various resistance groups, carrying information.

The Carpetbaggers dropped supplies and agents into occupied countries all along the Channel coast to help organize and set up more underground units as well as to send vital enemy troop movements and radio lists of needed supplies to the main office in London.

The OG's, who were also dropped by the Carpetbaggers, co-coordinated, directed and worked with the underground on their raids on the enemy. Later many of these men and women worked in the CBI (China, Burma, India) areas of the war in the Pacific. There was also the SO, know as Special Operations and SI, which was the Secret Intelligence.

The entire OSS was composed of volunteers. The records of all the men and women entering the service were checked to see if one had a particular talent that the OSS needed. This individual was then interviewed and offered the opportunity to volunteer for an interesting and risky adventure in a new outfit that was in the process of being formed or they could return to their present outfit. The ones being given this opportunity were often those fluent in a foreign language, radio or other electrical experience. They were then given a little background of the OSS and the briefing ended with these words, " you are not to talk of this outfit to ANY one! If you do you will be taken out and immediately SHOT!" As Joe LaMarre once told me after that there was NO WAY he was going to talk to any one about this outfit.

Today, many are still are leery about talking of these experiences even after 60 plus years and knowing that most activities of the OSS have been declassified.

Attending reunions with Jack I noticed many of the men sitting around talking and laughing so naturally I became curious and started eaves dropping and listened to their many tales. Following the reunions I would try to get Jack started talking about some of his experiences and found that was harder then finding that proverbial hen's tooth. As he started talking I quietly gathered his tales together and began writing about a few in the OSS COMM VETS newsletter. Since Jack had been a radio operator with the Carpetbaggers he was eligible for membership in several OSS Societies. I began to talk with other members and slowly gathered a fair number of their stories and James Ranney, Editor of the OSS COMM VETS began to enourage me to contact many others and put their stories in book form. Many of them were reluctant at first to open up and share their experiences, but using a little feminine charm and a little bit of guile I finally succeeded.

Let us remember these men, boys really, had never been far from home and most of them were probably between the ages of 18 and 20 something. Even the officers were between their middle to late 20's so we had a very young army and navy and hence, they all felt they were immortal. Few had any experience with death and as a result they were always ready to see the funny side of life. Many of the stories they tell today were not funny when they happened, but now as they have matured and look back they see the lighter side of their experiences

I was prompted to write this book as I had read that nearly 1000 Veterans are being daily taken from us by the "Grim Reaper" and taking their stories with them, as well as for my love for Jack and his crew and all the others who served in this risky and secret organization. The OSS was certainly the best-kept secret of WW II.

So now on to their stories.

CHAPTER 1
THE TALES OF TWO WOMEN

There were a goodly number of women who were members of the OSS, however I was only fortunate enough to have two who answered my requests. One served in the European theater and the other in the Pacific.

Elizabeth McIntosh, who wrote the "Sisterhood of Spies" used much of the information on women in her book, however she was kind enough to give me one that happened to her. After I read it I wondered how many times the words,"Don't tell anyone" comes back to haunt us. In McIntosh's case it resulted in her being transferred quickly to behind the lines in China.

McIntosh was on temporary duty in India, awaiting assigment to Kunming, China, along with five Nisei friends. The five friends had been students of McIntosh's mother in high school in Hawaii. One day when they all had leave they decided to take a trip to the Taj Mahal in Agra.

The day arrived sunny and beautiful and early in the morning they took off for Agra. As they were all from Hawaii they spent the time driving and singing Hawaiian songs (some she admits today were "naughty") Driving along singing they enjoyed the beauty of the country although the poverty they observed also made it rather dismal. Finally they arrived at this magnificent tomb and explored it for most of the afternoon. On their way out they asked one of the attendants at the shrine to take a picture of them with the marble dome in the background. Getting back to camp and thinking her mother would enjoy seeing all of them together she sent a copy of the picture with the warning that she couldn't tell her parents where they were as it would be a security violation.

Her father, who at the time happened to be sports editor on the Honolulu Advertiser, ran the picture on the front page of the paper. Two days later she and her friends were called in by security and given a stern lecture on violating security regulations. It didn't do any good to say she had warned her mother she couldn't tell her parents were they were. Five days later she and her friends were on their way to China. That was one way to get fast action.

Today McIntosh is editor of the OSS Society newsletter.

Another woman who served in the OSS started out as a WAC and sent me a booklet she had written regarding her experience in the OSS for her children. I feel she sat down and wrote it after hearing innumerable times, "What did you do during the war Mom?" She so vividly portrayed her life at that time that I not only enjoyed what she had written, but she also gave me permission to use as much as I wanted and I hope I can do it as vividly as she did. Elizabeth vonBakonyl didn't state her age at the time of Pearl Harbor, but afterwards she wanted to contribute to the war effort and decided the Navy was the way to go. Wait a minute, at the start of this I stated she was a WAC, so what changed her mind from Navy to Army? Read on. She felt the Navy would provide her with a chance of going to Europe and went to the recruiting office to enlist in the Waves. When she had filled out the forms and was told to step up and read the eye chart she responded with, "What chart?" and promptly washed out. The Marines and Army Air Force would have nothing to do with her either for the same reason as the Navy. The Army was less particular and let her keep her glasses on. It was smooth going, (I can't say sailing as this was the ARMY) until she came to the blood pressure part of the physical. This time her blood pressure was to low. She was about to cry when the medic, feeling sorry for her, told her to go and run around the block and come back for him to check it again. OLE! This time she passed the test.

She went through basic training and finally to Fort Oglethorpe where she continued to buck the system by volunteering every chance she had. Here, she met a girl whom like herself had relatives in Switzerland. They became long and lasting friends and both had a deep desire to go overseas.

After weeks of training that included the development of skills such as a standard response to the "abandon ship" order, swimming through imaginary boiling oil, donning gas masks within three seconds after the warning whistle was blown

And to pack and unpack "A" and "B" duffle bags on the double-until one night it all changed. It was almost time for bed check when she was called to the orderly room. She wondered what she was in for as no one was called at that time of the night for a minor infraction. Pictures of all type of all types of punishment went through her mind up to and including court martial. She reported on the double and arrived to find her Commanding Officer waiting for her and she thought she was REALLY in Dutch. The CO smiled (that relieved her) and told her to wait in the day room with the others. There they were, five lowly privates and one PFC. Finally a Lieutenant came into the room and told them to return to their quarters and to return in one hour, in uniform and with packed "A" and "B" bags.

In an hour they were back in the orderly room, with bags, shining shoes and brass and hair off of collars (sounds like orders for student nurses. No hair must touch collars). The PFC was handed sealed orders, they piled into a waiting personnel carrier and were off to the train station. Finally at 0300 hours (3 AM to us not used to that type of time) on an August morning in 1943 they found they had arrived at the Nation's Capital.

There the atmosphere was entirely different. They were finally in touch with the war. A sergeant whose password agreed with theirs met them and they were marched, in formation, through the main exit and ushered down into the cellar of "Q" building to report for duty in a huge bank vault with a table that could accommodate a larger number of people then the six bedraggled bunch of tired kids. A tough looking and grumpy sergeant, with an armload of stripes, informed them that all had been given top security clearance and they were now members of the intelligence section of the OSS. He told them that it was treason if they mentioned anything outside the vault as to where they were or what they were doing.

VonBakonyl went on to say two specially cleared officers took the secret codes and ciphers out of the vault and that automatic locks and secret combinations secured the vault. They learned the hand cipher system used by our agents to radio traffic from behind enemy lines. It was now that they learned the difference between our agents and enemy spies. After some weeks of working with a strict and sometimes grumpy sergeant that they learned they were to be transferred to another base. When the orders came through they learned it was overseas for the group.

Women of the OSS were essential office personnel, radio operators, handled code and also served as couriers. They were all a part of the "Sisterhood of Spies" that Elizabeth McIntosh so beautifully portrayed in her book under that title. They were in as much danger as all the men even though they were not in the forefront of battle.

VonBakonyl was one of these women. She was one of the groups of twelve women who sailed from Fort Lee, Virginia, wearing their summer khakis, only to find themselves heading into the North Atlantic. They were aboard a former Cunard liner, which had been converted into a troop ship. The twelve were quartered in first class luxury while the 3000 male troops were quartered below decks. The men were being sent to support the troops that Rommel, known as the Desert Fox, had cut to pieces. The women had no idea where they were headed after leaving the states until they landed at Casablanca in North Africa.

As they left the ship and drove off in what they called a "butt buster" which was a personnel carrier with wooden seats, they found their spirits rising as they as rode in the warm sun past pretty houses covered with burgundy vines. However, their spirits were quickly dampened as they reached their destination, which was a dismal, and isolated camp surrounded by a barbwire topped chain link fence. Here they were to be quarantined for three weeks. One thing she was grateful for however was that at least she wasn't seasick.

The next morning when they awoke most were shocked and terrified to find their faces swollen, lips thick and eyes half open. The WAC doctors were baffled and in desperation the women were load onto vehicles and taken on sight seeing drive while the doctors spent a frantic day communicating with the zone of the interior for instructions. The following morning the swelling in their faces had receded some and it seems they had been issued blankets that had been packed in some type of mothball preservative since WW I and they were allergic to it.

After three weeks they were given a five day supply of C rations and told to pack and soon found themselves on a miserable little ratty train chugging across the Atlas Mountains. They were sure that after five days of C rations they too, like the blankets were relics of that same war. Camaraderie grew out of this shared misery that touched of laughter, tears, humor, prayer and profanity.

At the first station stop the women were met by some Berbers, dressed in their traitional hooded burnooses, which had just been liberated from the Germans by American and English troops. They showered the women with huge baskets of oranges, which they passed through the windows. The women in turn gave them left over C rations and the Berbers received them with great joy. Hours later they arrived at a 20th century station and the sign told them they were in Algiers.

Here they were met by the army and driven to another building surrounded by a ten foot, barbed wire concrete wall. This was called School One and would be their quarters for the next few months. This had originally been the home for six wives of a lesser potentate and each wife had an elaborately tiled apartment.

While in Algiers vonBakonyl relates that the Algiers Opera was to produce the Opera Rigoletta and she and the other WAC's had signed up to go and were to be given transportation to and from the opera. The quartet from Rigoletta was in the last act and she wasn't about to miss it even if she was confined to quarters for a month. She told herself it was worth it as she sneaked out past the disapproving looks of the Algerians as she left before Gilda was dead and out on the street she knew any military vehicle would pick up a stranded WAC.

The first military vehicle that came along was carrying a load of sailors who had just landed and when the truck stopped they hauled her aboard. The driver knew the location of the WAC's quarters and they headed in that direction. On the way the sailors and vonBakonyl struck up a lively conversation when the lad next to her asked if she had taught science in Logan, West Virginia, he told her he had been in one of her classes. A chat of "back home" conversation took place. One never knows whom one will meet away from home. Thanks to these sailors she made bed check by the skin of her teeth.

There were many war torn kids through out Algiers. They lived in anything hollow and stole anything that wasn't nailed down. There was one, Mustafa who said he was ten, but looked more like six. He would appear out of nowhere and disappear just as quickly and had the street savvy of a Mafia agent. He hung around vonBakonyl and the other WAC's and would bring them dates, figs and green almonds and became their mascot. One day they sneaked him into the shower room, scrubbed him down, found him some decent clothes and supplied him with cigarettes that were legal tender on the black market. After that he would do anything for the women who called him, Musty.

When the troops landed on the beaches of Salerno the women knew they would soon be moved over into Italy also. This time they were sent to the AFHQ (Air Force Headquarters) at Caserta and they were billeted, thanks to Mussolini, in the fanciest barracks they had ever seen. The palace had wide windows and staircases.

With modern art and plenty of chrome as well as marble and crystal chandeliers. They did not work in the palace as their work was to hush-hush for that so each day they were taken to a tiny castle a couple of miles away, deep in a protective hunting woods.

Showing the difference in the meaning of words and culture vonBakonyl goes on to tell how one day she and a friend were on a shopping trip in Naples and stopped and a had a beer and talked to a Dominican monk who worked at an orphanage for boys whose parents had been lost in the war. During the course of conversation the monk told them the orphanage was terribly poor and strapped for food, clothing and textbooks. Naturally the two women wanted to know what they could do to help and were told the boys would dearly love to have a football. They told the monk they would check among the GI units they were familiar with and see what they could do. They found someone who knew an R&R (rest and recreation) supply sergeant who came up with a new football, which they couldn't wait to deliver. The news preceeded them and they were met by cheering kids, only to see their poor little faces drop to their knees, they had no idea what to do with the strange shaped pigskin. It was a soccer ball they really wanted. The women assured the kids that they would make good on their promise even though at that point they had no idea how they could do that. However, someone in the barracks had a friend in a Limey outfit that came across with a soccer ball and their Yankee honor was saved.

One of the women from the village, who did the laundry for the WAC's became quite friendly with vonBakonyl and several of the other women at the message center and invited them to Caserta Vecchia on Christmas Eve to see a play and have dinner with she and her family. On a prior visit to the village they had visited the Cathedral of San Michele where the play was to be held.

It was a freezing cold day when they arrived at the village and were met by the usual group of black-eyed children waiting for their ration of candy and gum. Maria, who had invited them, sent the children with them to find good seats. The town was beautifully decorated with lights and greenery and a friendly holiday spirit pervaded the whole town. When the dinner was ready Maria sent the children back to the cathedral to bring the women back to her house. The dinner was quite festive with roast goose, which I have been told is the tradional Christmas dinner in Europe. The dinner also included roast pork, winter vegetables, the unique Italian bread and plenty of Chianti. When they asked her how she could have produced such a meal they were told that the rations they had given her had been taken to black market friends and they produced anything she wanted.

Towards midnight, knowing they had to be back at the message center and on duty they regretfully took their leave. Up to this point the party had been the most charming and unique event they had attended, however the most devastating, unforgettable and terrifying encounter was yet to come.

The other guests begged them not to leave. The werewolf was always out on Christmas Eve and a full moon such as they had that night made the werewolf doubly dangerous. The women hated to leave the party even more at that point. They respected the werewolf, but they had a war to fight and they feared their "top kick" even more then the werewolf.

They finally tore themselves away from the group amid showers of tears, blessings, prayers, rosaries, and Hail Mary's and pagan chants. By this time they were developing their own private qualms and out on the street, in the shadow of the cathedral and the full moon the werewolf became a reality. One of them reported that the natives might be right as coming up that afternoon she had seen a shepherd whose dog had on a spiked collar to protect him from the werewolf. By this time they were outside the gates of the village, they took each other's hands and ignoring the road they ran straight down the hill. They were inside of the message center in San Leuccio with in fifteen minutes instead of the usual hour it took them to get there from the cathedral.

The next morning Maria came to the barracks and in tears threw herself at them and telling them that all of them in the house where the party had been held spent the night in prayer and that is why they had made it back safely. She went on to write that anyone who does not believe in werewolves has never been in Caserta Vecchia during a full moon on Christmas Eve.

Continuing on she wrote that she and a friend had a brief glimpse of what returning troops had been through when one afternoon they struggled up abandoned back trails to the top of a hill a couple of miles north of San Leuccia and decided to see what was on the other side of the hill. They had to hack their way through impossible terrain and shoulder high underbrush, vine and brambles. Two hours after breaking through all this they found themselves facing a field below. By this time they were terrified, but there was no turning back now. They had not been strafed so they continued on their way and when they found a huge holly tree they collected an armful and went on their way across a field and came to a road where they were cut off by barbed wire. Some way or another they maneuvered their way to the road and there they saw a huge "OFF LIMITS" sign. They stuck their thumbs up at the first GI vehicle that came along and were pulled aboard. When the GI's asked where they had gotten the holly they pointed to the field they had just come through. The men couldn't believe it as they told the girls they had just come through a minefield. If the guys had reported them they could have been court martialed. They didn't and they weren't and so the women came to the conclusion they lead charmed lives.

At that time General Patton was barreling across France, the Ramagen Bridge, the Alsace and Germany and the message center was was sizzling and buzzing with messages. There were always discussions as to how long the Germans could hold out and the white flags would be hoisted. VonBakonyl tells about meeting a charming titled woman who told her that she had the deplorable task of waving the white flag in her area. She went on to say she didn't know which was worse; waving that white sheet surrendering her town or having the elasatic in her war worn underwear break while she was doing it

CHAPTER 2
FROM SARDINIA TO ITALY

T he son of another OSS member sent the following experience
of Anthony Camboni to me. This son had married into the
family of Mr. Camboni and he had sent it to his father to give to
me.

A Mr. Earl Brennan, who was head of the OSS Italian Section,
called on Anthony Camboni at his home one day in early 1942. He
asked Camboni if he was willing to join an organization, which
was being formed for intelligence duty in Italy. The first thing that
popped into his mind was, "Why me?" Camboni was 43 years old
at that time, married and had two small boys. The answer was that
he had been recommended as a person qualified first by birth, his
knowledge of the language and his political activity and had been
advised that Camboni could head-up such a mission.

Camboni was a militant anti-fascist, who had been born in
Sardinia, knew the language and dialects as well as many of
the inhabitants. He was also a member of the Italian Freedom

Organization whose purpose was to make Italy a United Republic. His activities with the Italian Socialist Federation of the U. S.A. made him a natural enemy of facism, Mussolini and Naziism. So before agreeing to the request he talked it over with a Professor Borgese, who taught at the Chicago University and Count Sforza, who had been Ambassador to France and resigned when Mussolini took office. After talking with these two men Camboni did volunteer for this risky duty as he felt that any effort he could make to help the country of his birth and alleviate the oppression of the Italian people was good.

In his particular section there were about twenty five volunteers at first, but a few of them decided it was to risky and dropped out. The men who did not make the mission were sent to Italy after the capitulation of Mussolini and worked with the military government.

Five men were chosen for this mission and were sent to Sparks, Maryland for twelve weeks of training. Their instructors were FBI members and British counter-espionage experts and their group was known as Secret Intelligence. Here at Sparks they were taught the use of firearms, mortars, and photography among other things. As part of their exercise they were sent, individually, to a another town (Baltimore?) to purchase narcotics, break into and burglarize homes and apartments during which time Camboni nearly got shot so the town was declared "Out of bounds". They also had a limited course in navigation and disguises. They were re-indoctrinated in Italian table manners, which are different from American, were required to act as the native Italians do so that they might not be conspicuous in

Italy. These I can assure you are very noticeable in European cities and immediately tell the natives that you are not from the area. This was brought home to us when we lived in Germany.

The middle of June, 1943 found the men in Algiers and here they practiced landing PT boats. They learned they were to be sent to Sardinia and Camboni was placed in charge. On the 28th of June the men went to Bone and again made two more practice landings and left Bone around noon on the 30th on the PT boat, Zamba, with two other PT boats as escorts. A Lieutenant Corvo and Captain Passenesi accompanied the party to see that their disembarkation went along smoothly. The presence of the two officers of course gave the men more confidence and during the voyage they had final discussions about their security and safety and how to proceed after their landing.

Their mission was to land on the coast below Monte Mannu and there to contact natives and to report back by radio such intelligence that they might be able to obtain. They arrived at what they thought was their destination shortly before midnight, July 1st. The PT boats stopped a short distance from shore and they put their equipment in a rubber boat and started to paddle to shore. The sea had been calm, but became rougher as they neared the shore. The night was very dark and there wasn't a moon. They appeared to be landing at the foot of a high cliff and just before reaching shore there was a flash of light on the cliff that appeared to be like a glow of a room, as if a door had been opened and closed. They later found out that the light was an Italian outpost. The two PT boats left them as they continued to paddle towards shore trying to find a good landing place when the surf suddenly caused them to be thrown from the boat into the water, but their life belts saved them.

Upon landing they found nothing but rocks with a high cliff above them and it was obvious that any more traveling that night was out of the question. However they wouldn't give up and started climbing the dangerous terrian, very carefully and in a spiral manner, resting now and then to make reconnaissances. At the top of the cliff they found that there was no passage into the interior except by a small dangerous path. The path was covered by rock protrusions, which necessitated crawling on their stomachs. Since there was no alternative one of the men volunteered to use this path to the top. This man, Puleo by name, made it to the top, made a brief reconnaissance and seeing no one, helped the others get their equipment up the cliff. They walked for about half of a kilometer and found a place to rest. By this time it was 1930 hours (7:30 PM). They continued and saw some telephone wires and a small thatched hut that appeared to be the sort of shelter used by shepherds in outlying fields.

They quietly approached the hut and Camboni seeing a few soldiers called out, "Hello Italians." and the soldiers replied cordially, but did not realize who they were. Camboni told them that they were lost and were told they were near Punta Furana and was told that Alghero was to the south. He realized then that they had landed a good deal further up the coast than their original destination. One of the soldiers asked if they had come from Tunsia amd Camboni told the soldiers that yes they had and that they had had an accident and were going to Sassari. They were offered bread and water, which they refused and took off in the direction given them.

They walked another kilometer and a half and saw another outpost and decided to wait here because although the soldiers at the first outpost had not appeared suspicious, there was always the possibility that they might be stopped. As they were resting some soldiers suddenly appeared and asked them what they were doing. Having told them they were eating the soldiers apparently didn't believe them as they were ordered to come out with their arms up. They were disarmed and returned to the post from which they had come. They left their equipment, including the radio, hidden in the bushes.

A Corporal in charge who by now knew they were Americans questioned the men. About midnight a Major arrived with about 25 soldiers with machine guns and later an even larger detachment arrived. When the Major interrogated Camboni he said, " You speak better Italian and Sardinian then I do and you can tell that crippled President of yours we are ready for the American Army." Camboni protested the insult and the Major half apologized. They were then taken by truck to Porto Torres where they were stripped of everything they had and interrogated again with Camboni acting as interpreter and gave no information other then names and serial numbers.

They were taken to Bortigali and placed in separate cells and on the morning of July 4th they were handcuffed and taken by truck to Sassari and placed in San Sebastiano prison. Here they stayed until

July 23rd and then taken to Gerolamo Bellinguerra Station where most of the guards were Sardinians and as a result things began to improve. The men gained the confidence of the Sardinian guards who in turn gave Camboni and the others information about their families and friends. After gaining the confidence of the guards the men began a psychological campaign by telling them of their futility in fighting a war that was not popular with the Italian people. They repeatedly told them that the Americans had no hard feelings towards the Italian people and that about ten million Italians were living in America and were proud to be there in a free democratic country.

On the morning of July 26th the major came and awakened them to tell them of the fall of Mussolini. After several days they were taken to Sassari where they were liberated and given civilian clothes. Around the middle of September they were ordered to Macomer where they met Colonel Obolensky (a Russian Count who worked with the OSS. We will hear more about him later) along with a US General Theodore Roosevelt, Jr. By the time these two gentlemen arrived this small group had already made contact with the OSS in Algiers,

In spite of the fact that they landed in the wrong spot and taken prisoners shortly after they landed their mission was a success. The mission made the first contact between the Allies and the Forze of Armata of Sardinia.

This story of Camboni gives another side of the war that is not often described or discussed so I've included it in the book.

And now to continue in this area of the world we go to Italy and one evening there in the life of Captain James Hudson who was in SI- (Secret Intelligence) and played a big part in the rescue of thirteen US Air Force nurses who crash-landed in the Albanian mountains while the Germans occupied the country. With the help of British Intelligence agents and the OSS the nurses were able to escape. Captain Hudson was the commanding officer of SEAVIEW, a cave on the Adriatic coast used during the escape. He also served with the OSS in the Middle East as the photographic censor of the armed forces in that area. But now on with his story.

In March of 1944 Hudson was trying to infiltrate from Otranto, Italy into the coast of Albania. Sterling Hayden of the OSS Special Operations and Hollywood's gift to the OSS on a fishing boat, Yankee, piloted him. They took off about sundown and headed east on the Adriatic. It was quite calm and they anticipated an easy voyage, but the sea can be treacherous and quickly became choppy and finally turned into a roaring storm. They lost all of their supplies that had been lashed down on the deck and barely made it back to the tiny port of Otranto.

They headed for a very small town looking for food and drink. At 3 AM everything was closed and dark. Finally they found a tavern and noisily awakened the owner and demanded he open up for them. He did and they ate and drank until they were satiated. They maybe even had more vino (wine) then was necessary, as the rest remains foggy in their minds.

How and why they went their separate ways looking for a friendly house in which to spend what was left of the night remains unclear. How Hayden made out Hudson never asked, but apparently he found a small hovel and fell fast asleep. The next morning a very large and very unhappy lady awakened him. The language barrier kept them from understanding each other, but Hudson soon got the impression that she would be much happier if he would vacate the premises and the sooner the better. Why she didn't kill him and how he got to her house only God knows, but he sheepishly made his exit and made it down to the dock where he finished his nap.

He never did say what the out come of this mission was or where Hayden spent the night or how they were able to get back together again. He leaves us "hanging" and perhaps some day he will give us the end of this tale in one of his books. I hope so as I hate to be left "hanging".

Another Italian experience comes from Albert Materazzi. He was a chemist specializing in lithograpy and photography and had been working for the Army Map Service for two years before joining the army in June 1942. He then taught lithography at the Engineer School until March 1943. At that time he was called in for an interview by a Major Russell Livermore who had been assigned by General Donovan to organize the Operational Groups (OG's). The General felt that given the ethnic richness of the U.S he could recruit a couple hundred to drop behind the enemy lines to foster armed resistance movements and hoped as Churchill had said to "set Europe ablaze". Landings in Italy were imminent and that country was a priority and Engineers who had been trained in demolitions were especially needed. Materazzi wrote me that his group was the first Operational Group formed and spent 23 months in the Mediterrian area and their primary mission was to assist resistance forces of the partisans, but were also used as commandos at times.

To this day Materazzi is not sure if he volunteered or not, but several weeks later he along with five other 2nd lieutenants were ordered to the Adjutant General's office in Washington and he found out he HAD joined the OSS along with the four other men and were the first OG's and today are considered as the forerunners of the Special Forces.

A year later found them in Corsica conducting commando type operations against the Ligurian coast. In April of 1945 the final campaign in Italy began and General Mark Clark, commanding the fifteenth Army Group, was concerned that it would not be possible for regular army forces to get to Bolzano in time to prevent General Karl Wolfe, commander of the SS Forces, from the destruction of valuble documents and records and prevent post armistice partisan attacks. A special mission commanded by Colonel Russell B Livermore (this was the same Major Livermore who first interviewed Materazzi in April of 1943 in Washington.) who was the CO of the 2671 Special Reconnaissance Battalion, representing the OSS and included representatives of the British SOE (Special Operations Executive and similar to our OSS) and the Allied Commission, which could move rapidly and take over the German facilities. Livermore chose Materazzi as his aide.

The convoy left Verona early on the morning of May 4th and arriving at Bolzano at dusk with crowds of Italians cheering them on as they made their triumphal entry. The next day while at dinner, Materazzi's driver rushed in and said, "Captain, come quick, the war is about to start over." The driver handed Materazzi his pistol and they ran to the nearby square and found a skirmish line of Italian partisans opposing a group of Germans on trucks to be transported to POW camps. Many were on trucks originally belonging to Italy and the partisans did not want the Germans on those trucks. Materazzi was able to convince them that since the war were still going on up north they had to get the Germans out of the Alps to the POW camps in the Po valley.

Soon Colonel Livermore arrived with the acting Prefect of Bolzano. It turned out that the partisans had been sent to assist returning POWs streaming over the Brenner Pass for which provisions had already been made. The Prefect had made arrangements to feed and house them in a nearby school overnight.

At this point two members of the partisans came forward and said they were from Bolzano and had heard that the Germans were occupying the farm of one of them and the other had an apartment that the Germans had occupied and he was worried about his wife and daughter. The Colonel called for his command car and the two partisans, the Prefect and Materazzi went to the farm where they found a company of Germans. Materazzi translated the Colonels orders into Italian and the Prefect translated them into German. As they were leaving the Colonel noticed a radio and asked if it was

German issue and upon hearing it had been "requisitioned" in the south the Colonel took it. They then headed to the apartment and by then the Germans knew they coming and were on their way out, you can imagine the happy reunion between the partisan and his family and out came the wine with which to toast the Americans. The Colonel noted there was no radio so he had his driver bring the one in the car into the apartment. As they were leaving, the Colonel (who was a lawyer) winked at Materazzi and said, "it might not be legal, but justice has been done."

CHAPTER 3
MORE FROM THE OG'S

I mentioned the OG's in the previous chapter, but didn't go into much detail about them. OG's were small self sufficient teams composed of any where from fifteen to thirty men, who were trained in demolition, sabotage, hit and run raids, how to gather information and return it to London as well as the organization of local men into groups of guerrilla forces called the Marquis. A good number of them were fluent in the language of the country into which they jumped. Some who did not speak the language were taken into groups because they were skilled in radio or they were medics.

Many OG's in the states were trained at the Congressional Club outside of Washington, DC where they really had it good. Tom McGuire writes that they had no KP or guard duty, but did have a lot of night training. However lets go back to the original reason Tom had for joing the OSS.

McGuire was drafted in February of 1943and he signed up for the paratroopers and went to Camp Taccoa in Georgia. Here he washed out because of an old football injury that began to act up. He was assigned to 134th Infantry, B Company in California. It was here that his Captain received a letter from McGuire's mother asking when her son would be promoted to A Company. He laughingly told me, "This didn't sit to well with the Captain.

Here McGuire tells the tale that in the Paratroops the fellows always bloused their pants over the top of their boots using rubber bands to hold them. When they were overseas many times they could not get their hands on rubber bands so they often resorted to the use of condoms. He goes on to say that if they saw a jumper coming back to camp after a leave without his pants bloused they knew (and I quote) "that he'd had a hellva time on leave"

When he was at Camp Buckner, NC a Major Camp was sent to interview him as he was looking for volunteers (as he said) for hazardous duty. Seems some one had found out he could read and speak French. "Yeh Hazardous" said McGuire later in life. He had what he thought was a good reason for joining the OSS at that time. The increase in pay and a promotion. He had an allotment for his mother who was a widow and with laundry and insurance he was drawing $17.00 per month. He was promised a promotion to corporal, which was a raise of $12.00 plus $50.00 for jump pay so he immediately volunteered.

He was sent to the Congressional Country Club for training for a short period of time and soon left from Newport News, Virginia in a convoy of 1000 ships and sailed to Casablanca. There they

26

boarded the famous 40 & 8 box cars and traveled on to Algiers. While in Algiers there was more night training and 4 jumps to be made in order to qualify for the "big money!" At the end of May two French Groups under the command of Colonel Obolensky sailed for England.

Colonel Obolensky was the crown prince of Russia who had served in the Russian Army. A good book to read if interested in this man is "One Man in His Time" written by Obolensky telling his life story and is most interesting and fascinating.

Once some one gets McGuire talking he can go on for hours and never tells the same tale twice. He tells that before leaving Algiers for England everyone exchanged his North African franc notes for British currency. While at sea on their way over to England one officer went to the "head" and being short of paper used what he thought was a one pound note, only later to find out it had been a five pound worth $20.00 in American money. I'll bet he cried in his beer later in the day after they landed.

Another story he tells, which I cannot verify, but McGuire swears is true and after reading it you decide. He wrote me that all OG's and SO's (English groups?) who jumped into enemy territory were given an escape kit containing a cloth map (Jack tells me they were silk), French and American money, an extremely hard file and a compass the size of a dime in diameter and four dimes in thickness. If after jumping and using the compass it became necessary to hide it and you had large nostrils you could hide the compass in your nose. If not there was only one alternative hiding place was then classified as an a--hole compass.

The story is told of one OG who had to hide the compass in his escape. He returned to England and was debriefed. He said everything was OK, but later he had a small problem when in England. He said he could be standing on a street corner and all at once his rear end would start to twitch to the North. Believe it or not-it's up to you.

This is another one that McGuire came up with. While they were in France they found a lot of good barns in which they could have slept in at night, but Colonel Obolensky had other ideas and insisted they stay in the woods at night. Another order he issued was that they were not to go into town at night. Naturally human nature always reacts to an order like that and of course some of the men slipped out and mingled with the locals. One morning the Colonel was surprised when one of the locals rushed up, embraced him saying, "I love you so much I'm constipated!" The guys had taught him this phrase and I wonder what type of punishment was meted out to the guilty and if McGuire played a part in the education of the local men.

McGuire was a part of the "Patrick Mission" in France where they were to help assist all resistance groups in protecting a highly important hydroelectric power station at Eguzon. Whenever they could they were to conduct attacks on rail, road and communication targets. In other words they were to harass and pester the Germans with their hit and run raids.

This group arrived in France on August 16 and completed their mission and shipped back to England arriving on September 13th and were shipped back to the States and were given a months leave over Christmas of 1944. They were then shipped from California to India. Colonel Obolensky did not go with them because of his age and the group was under the command of Captain John Cook. They rode across all of India on a train and finally wound up in Calcutta. From there they drove over the Burma Road to Kunming. Many of the men had never driven trucks before and these were British vehicles with right hand drive and towing a 37mm cannon and loaded with ammunition. The first thing they did was to remove the right hand door for a quick exit because of the narrow roads.

After their arrival outside of Kunming they began training the Chinese in the use of the rifle. On July 27th they dropped with the 2nd Chinese Commandos in what was called "Operation Blueberry". The group attacked the Japanese on August 5th at Tai-Yuan-Tzu and the war ended shortly after that.

Rob Drew, whose father, Larry, fought with McGuire in the Chinese theater sent me the following story. His father remembered the humor as well as the horror of the war, but chose mostly to share the humor. Now the son did not tell me if this happened with a group his Dad was with or if it had been one that his Dad had heard but anyway it is a good one.

Drew was on Guadalcanal with the 25th division before joining the OSS.

All the people volunteering for the OSS were not only interviewed, but they were also given psychologist evaluation by a panel of psychologists. One outstanding candidate was asked several questions when one asked him if he dreamed of making love to his mother. The potential OSSer looked stunned for a moment, then stood and picked up the psychologist and hurled him into the simming pool. (Let's hope there was water in the pool-my comment) later the OSS officers told him this incident hadn't disqualified him, but the candidate politely replied that he didn't think the OSS was the right place for him and he felt more at home in the regular army. The next day he returned to his unit and later distinguished himself with Patton in Europe.

Like Drew, I wondered what the esteemed psychologist hoped to hear.

CHAPTER 4
COMMUNICATIONS

C ommunicating with others is a most important aspect in
our lives, but during wartime it is most vital for the troops
to communicate with each other. This can be done using hand
signals, flags, hand held "crickets", code, radio, flares, and the
Navajo Indians devised a code they from their language which the
Japanese never were able to decode. The Germans used the enigma
machine and after the Americans were able to obtain one and were
able to break the code it became a valuable tool for the Americans.
Here again you can see how valuable an OSS person who was
fluent in a foreign language was to an outfit. You could find these
people working with all the branches of the OSS.

Ralph Tibbetts was just that type of person. James Ranney, editor
of the OSS COMM VETS newsletter, has given me permission to
use an article that Tibbetts had written for the newsletter in March
of 1997. Tibbetts is now deceased, but Ranney, who knew him well,

felt that Tibbetts would have been very pleased to know his article was being used. This is to honor him and all the rest who were a part of Detachment 101 serving in the China, Burma, and India Theater. So here's to you Tibbetts and all the rest who served over there.

When Tibbetts was sixteen years of age he enlisted in the National Guard, but two years later when the Guard was federalized he was given an honorable discharge due to the fact that he was blind in one eye. So here he was, eighteen years of age and a PFC. He enlisted in the RAF through a British agent with the Cunard White Star Line in Boston.

After a year of training in Canada and having married, it looked as though the US would get into the war so he was given another discharge and told to return to his own country and enlist in the USA. Back home he went to Raytheon Company to work as a radar tech. So here he was, back home, a radar tech with a pregnant wife and lo and behold he was DRAFTED! He was sent to what is now Fort Deven, given a carbine, three cartridges and three Italian POW's to guard. As Tibbetts said in his article and I quote, " Heck, they weren't going anywhere; they never had it so good, cutting grass, sweeping sidewalks and bumming cigarettes."

One morning at roll call a sergeant asked if there were any men with radio or television experience. Several hands went up including his. They were ordered to don class A uniforms and report to the Provost Marshall. There he found around fifteen or twenty other guys milling around and asking questions, but getting no answers. Finally he was interviewed by a Captain who asked some dumb questions (as Tibbetts called them) and then asked if he would volunteer for hazardous duty and according to him he answered (and again I quote) " Hell, Sir, I'm in the Army and go where I'm sent." This must have been the right answer, as he says, as he was dismissed and sent out the back door and found himself escorted by two MP's to his barracks. Here he packed his duffle bag and proceeded, still under guard, to a completely empty barrack and was told he was not going ANY WHERE except with a guard. About now he was beginning to wonder, "What in the hell have I gotten myself into now?" After a few days he was awakened about 3 AM and told he was shipping out. He and the other men were put into a truck, the canvas was pulled down and they were driven from Base to Warner Robbins, Georgia and to the train depot. Here he was given an envelope, which contained the information that he was to report to the OSS at a certain address in Washington, DC. Now I quote him again, "WHAT IN THE HELL IS THE OSS? Service and Supply? Laundry? Office of Sloppy Sailors?" and he began to think he'd done it again and all he could do was try to get some sleep.

The next morning he grabbed a cab and went to the address on the envelope and found it was a brown building with two civilian guards at the door. They told him no one would there until 8 AM, but he could leave his baggage and could get some breakfast at the Deli at the end of the block. At the Deli while talking with the waitress he asked about the building down the street and was told, "that's a bunch of spies." and he thought he had really gotten his foot in it this time for sure. After breakfast he reported back to that "building of spies" and was interviewed again and since he couldn't type he was sent to a lab where he worked with a Dr. Morgan designing and building OSS gear.

Then he opened his mouth at the wrong time and embarrassed a Colonel, an ex-RCA engineer, who was showing some VIP's around the lab. Tibbetts and one other lab tech had had a few beers to many the night before and were somewhat hung over and didn't realize the lab door was open. The Colonel had made a remark about having been in the ETO (European theater of operations) and under fire. Tibbetts said and I quote, "He got that ribbon because he took his wife and kids on vacation.... And had never seen action."

Now that was really a BIG MISTAKE! The door closed and then opened again and the Colonel said, "I've decided to ship you out". There was a big globe on a stand in the room and he walked over to it and jabbed his finger down on it and said, "You are going HERE." He was pointing to China and that was the end of fun and games in DC.

Tibbetts was sent for further training to Area C which was located in what is now known as Prince William National Forest at Triangle, Virginia and not to far from Quantico, Virginia. It had formerly been a Civilian Conservation Camp (CCC) created by President Franklin Roosevelt to provide jobs during the depression. The location is in a heavily wooded area and today would be considered in the "boonies". There was a small creek running through it and the area was used as a rifle range. One day Tibbetts and about nine or ten others were undergoing weapons training when a flock of wild turkeys flew through the valley. The command was given to fire at will and the entire group qualified and they ate turkey for a week.

From Area C the group was put on a train for Cincinnati, Ohio and on the way the train was sidetracked and forgotten about for several days. There they were, no food, no orders…. Lost! Each of them had a Colt 45 and fifty rounds of ammunition so they did a little horse-trading to get money for food. Finally the railroad people found them and the troop car found it's way to California and a troop ship. Thirty days later they landed in Perth, Australia.

Tibbetts said all he remembered about the trip was that bunks were stacked eight high and the aisles were only two feet wide. The chow line never stopped; it ran twenty four hours a day and he never knew if he was in the breakfast or the supper line.

The good ladies of Perth decided to have a big welcoming party for their new comrades in arm and the ship's Captain accepted the invitation to the party. He began marching this dirty, ragged, smelly and very thirsty GI's down to a soccer field surrounded by a ten-foot wall. They had marched right through the middle of town and it seemed there was a pub on every corner. Naturally the lines thinned out as they marched and once they reached the field some one discovered a large hole in the fence created by the local kids and many others escaped this way.

Outside of the fence they ran into a couple of Aussies changing American dollars into English pounds. Tibbetts had his RAF experience to fall back on and knew the correct exchange rate. He grabbed another fellow and hooked a ride to the next town and here they began to lubricate their very dry livers and got glorious drunk. They finally decided it was time to return to the ship and the only way they could get aboard was to walk along bumper logs and steal over the rail. From there the ship sailed to Calcutta, India

When he finally arrived in Kunming, China he noticed a bunch of Chinese coolies repairing the runway and several jeeps nearby so he decided to "borrow" one as he had a master key. How he was able to get this master key is another story and best not to go into at this time. Anyhow, he "borrowed" the best looking jeep and decided a sight seeing tour of the city was in order. He found the tour most interesting, but wondered why at every intersection the Chinese police stopped all traffic and waved him on. After a most enjoyable tour he found his way back to where he had found the jeep and parked it in line with the rest. Walking past the front of the jeep he noticed eagles on each fender. With a big sigh of relief he walked off and found his way to the OSS compound feeling very relieved that his little side trip hadn't gotten him into any problems.

This was the end of his chronicles and left me wondering what else the rest of his of his tour of duty in China had been like.

Roy Lange wrote that three days after graduation from high school he was drafted and the Army selected the Signal Corp training for him. After arriving at Fort Monmouth, New Jerset, a regimental meeting was held and after introductions to persons unknown to them they were invited to volunteer for an assignment not related to the regular army. His father, a veteran of World War I, had always told him to never volunteer for anything in service. A buddy of his insisted they do so and both signed up for the unkown duty. Lange was selected, but his buddy wasn't and when he asked the sergeant why his buddy wasn't selected he was told in no uncertain terms not to question anything and found himself on his way to Washington, DC. During the trip they found they were headed for assignment with the OSS-what ever that was.

On arrival in Washington an orientation meeting was held and they found out to some extent what their assignment would be. They were supposed to be trained and dropped behind enemy lines in France and work in communications with the Frence underground. The Free French in England objected to this so they were sent to Fort McDowell in Illinois until they all received security clearence.

Needless to say when Lange's family and neighbors were questioned by the security people calls to his family, neighbors and friends began wanting to know what sort of mischief Lange had gotten himself into and   brought fast and furious letters to him. Naturally Lange was very limited in what he could tell his parents except that he was not in trouble. Once security was completed he was sent to Area C in Virginia for further training after which he was sent to a Base near Peterborough, England before being sent to France.

He had no idea how much weight the OSS carried with other service people. One day he was communicating from an Army position when he was approached by an officer of the unit who questioned him about his equipment and its capabilities. The officer went on to suggest that he might be inclined to attach him to his unit to meet his communications needs. When Lange replied he was with the OSS the officer replied, " carry on" and walked off.

Lange went on to tell about a memorable stop he and his lieutenant made at the 8th Infantry Division Headquarters. They had pulled up on a one-lane road outside of headquarters and he waited while the lieutenant went inside to gather information on their position. Hearing a horn behind him he immediately started up the jeep and pulled over to allow passage for the car behind him. Next he saw somebody standing beside the jeep demanding to know his name and outfit. Lange went on to say that all he could see were two pearl handed pistols and he Believe he must have broken all records getting out of the jeep and standing at attention because the man questioning him was none other then General Patton and riding with him was General Eisenhower. He blurted out his name and outfit and expected the worst. His infraction was failure to have the jeep windshield folded down and covered with a canvas sleeve to prevent reflection of the windshield to enemy aircraft. Immediately down came the windshield and covered. Happily he never heard anymore about the incident.

He had another interesting tale about entering Paris along with French troops. He and another jeep of communications men were authorized to enter Paris along with the French to identify their agents who had been working in the city.

Lange says it was like a big parade with the French soldiers being greeted by the people lined up along the street and throwing flowers at them. The people assuming them to be French began asking questions and of course they had to answer "no compree". The questions followed as to whether they were English? Canadian? And finally American? That touched off a huge response and their jeeps were essentially escorted into the city. A decision was made that in order to protect their equipment they would spend the night at a convent located near Place de Italy. After a meal served by the nuns, a priest went into a small flower garden and unearthed three bottles of vintage champagne that he had vowed not to unearth until Paris was liberated. Lange says if he remembers correctly that was his first taste of champagne.

A most unusual and bazaar tale came from John DiBlasi. It was classified until recently when John Brunner, another OSS man, told DiBlasi that it was now declassified and that this experiment was never carried forward into war as the war with Japan had ended before it could be used.

The name of project was Javaman and the way DiBlasi tells it the tale is funny, but back when it took place it could have ended up as a disaster for the people involved. It was the first air to guided missile system. A PT boat had a TV camera on the bow of the boat and a transmitter to relay the pictures to a TV receiver in the nose of a B-17. The boat a had an infrared searchlight. The controller in the nose of the air craft had a VHF transmitter that could send coded messages to a receiver in the boat for throttle-control, search light scan, rudder control, engine on and off and the last was "Blast the bottom out of the boat."

The idea behind the project was to guide several of these boats to the southern most islands of Japan where there were iron and coal mines and was a shipping point for these products to the north and the steel mills. The Japanese had built a tunnel between these islands and it supported rail and highway traffic to the mainland of Japan. The water between Honshu and Kyushu was relatively shallow-no more then 200 feet.

The plan was to sail several of these boats to the strait over the tunnel area. When the boats were in position over the tunnel the sailors who had guided the boats into position would jump overboard and be picked up by a submarine. The boats were then under control of the aircraft and the pilot would then hit the switch and the bottoms out of the boats and they would sink to the bottom of the sea. When the boats sank to the bottom the pressure sensitive switches would ignite the tons of explosives that were in the bottom of the boats and the concussioon of this tremendous explosion would be enough to destroy the tunnel.

Now lets have DiBlasi tell the story of his experience of a test run of this device.

While DiBlasi was stationed at Area C, in Virginia, he became quite friendly with another radio operator and they were picked for a special assignment and were told to report for transportation to their assignment. At this point they had no idea what the field task would be.

On arrival at Little Creek Mine Depot an OSS officer met and greeted them and at that time explained the test in which they were to take part. He told them that it would be a test of a new system that the OSS thought had merit for the naval section of the OSS and would be an asset in winning the war. He then began to explain what has previously been written, DiBlasi and his buddy were to be the radiomen aboard the boat and their job was to see that the system was operating correctly and in the event of any problems they might have they would then relay the information to the aircraft and follow their directions.

When they boarded the the torpedo boat they found a navy bo'suns mate assigned to the boat and his job was to see that the engine and controls were working properly and that all systems were go.

They checked out the communications gear and after letting the aircraft know they were ready they received the command to shove off and headed for open water. Up to this point the bo'sun had control of the boat, but upon receiving od\rders from the controller of the plane he locked on to the remote controls and the aircraft was in complete control of the boat. The controller aboard the aircraft was navigating their boat by the TV camera images he received.

They made several turns to test the response on the aircraft's directions and all seemed to be going smoothly. At this time they were running on 1/3 throttle and then received command to go full throttle. Full spead ahead!

The three Packard engines gave out a mighty roar and a blast of black smoke. The bow seemed to leap out of the water and they began picking up speed. They were now traveling about 50 miles per hour and DiBlasi said, "On water that's fast!". It became harder and harder to stand erect and every wave that they hit knocked them off their feet and they were holding on for dear life. If they had to make a quick correction it would have been almost impossible. As DiBlasi goes on he asks us to picture this scenario.

Here comes this torpedo boat, traveling at top speed and heading for the broadside of the navy cruiser and aiming for her midship section. The sailors aboard the cruiser started to get worried. Was this a bunch of nuts or were they drunk? Were they going to sink them right in the harbor? They could see the sailors running around the cruiser, waving their arms and trying to signal the boat away.

DiBlasi, his buddy and the bo'sun were depending on the aircraft operator to turn the boat in time, but there was some lag in the system and at the speed they were traveling they would surely hit the cruiser and there would probably be a loss of life aboard the cruiser as well as on the torpedo boat. By this time the men were no longer able to stand and sank to their butts.

We can imagine the commander aboard the cruiser sending out messages,"Sink that damn torpedo boat before it sinks my cruiser!".

They made another pass at the cruiser and closing in fast when they received the message to disengage and take over manually. They were being so badly battered about that night that neither DiBlasi nor his buddy could reach the controls and comply. Fortunately the bo'sun had been alert and saw the imminent disaster approaching and he was able to jump to the controls and yank the throttle shut and take over the control of the boat. Orders from the aircraft were to cease and return to Little Creek. The navy man took over the boat and all the way back they could hear him mumbling, "what numbskulls thought up this hair brained idea?". They never heard any more of this project.

DiBlasi says no more about this experience, but we find him being shipped to the Far East via Cairo and from there to Bombay, India. During the trip the he contracted pneumonia and ended up for two weeks in the hospital. While he was in the hospital the rest of his group shipped out and he ended up taking the famous Punjab Express and crossed India to Calcutta.

After about five days in Calcutta he and about twenty others were put on a plane to fly the hump to Kunming, China. The plane carried gasoline, a jeep or two and boxes of ammunition along with the GI's. As they boarded the plane DiBlasi saw there were about eight buckets in the center aisle of the plane and he couldn't imagine what they were for, however he soon found out. As they started their climb over the peaks of the high mountain it became evident by the color of faces of the men that those pails were going to serve a very useful purpose. After landing in Kunming all twenty men got down on their knees, kissed the ground and thanked their Almighty for their safe arrival.

DeBlasi was sent to a field station in the interior of China and behind Japanese lines. Here the men were to collect information from Chinese agents who were monitoring Japanese shipping and troop movements. Thie information was then evaluated and sent back to Kunming and the Air Force would then send fighters or bombers to take care of the situation.

At this station they were housed in an old Buddhist monastery with crumbling walls and wooden idols. Here the bad or non-existent roads along with food were a big problem. Captain Frillman was an old China hand having been the Padre of the famous Flying Tigers and he would locate and bargain for food. Water buffalo was the main source of meat, but smaller pieces were suspected to be cat, dog or even rat. If there was enough sauce they were able to get it down, but keeping it down was another story. Rice was the mainstay and when they first landed and found bugs in the cooked rice they wouldn't eat it. However, after a couple of months and becoming more hungry each day they would pick out the foreign matter and go on eating. After about eight months a person would simply close his eyes and eat.

Fresh fish was hard to get and one day some one had a great idea as to how to secure fish. They told the cook and coolies to go down to the water and wait about ten minutes, wade into the water and wait for the fish to magically appear. During the ten minutes the party down stream was waiting the GI's would be about ½ mile upstream and tossing several fragmentation grenades into the river. The blast would stun the fish and they would begin to float belly up down stream to where the cook and the coolies picked up the dazed fish and the GI's would have a feast that evening. This again shows American ingenuity at work.

The war was winding down and one day Diblasi and the rest of the group received word that they would be pulling out. They packed and preceded by whatever means they could muster to get to Shanghi, the OSS headquarters. I will not go into details of how they got to Shanghi, but good old American smarts played a big part. The navy arrived and they all received their back pay so things were looking up.

Beinging a radioman DiBlasi began operating the radio station there and reached an old friend in Formosa. This fella was unhappy as he had enough points to be rotated home when he was shipped to Formosa. He told DiBlasi that if he could get a replacement he would be shipped home. Good old soft hearted DiBlasi volunteered to replace him and he arrived at Taihoku, the capital of Formosa, his friend showed him the ropes and introduced to the commander, a Major Morgan.

Formosa was and still is a beautiful island with mountains, lush valleys, beautiful sheashore and pagodas. Major Morgan had taken over a Geisha House in the mountains of Hokuto to keep it from falling into the hands of Chinese officals. He told them that he needed it for high-level meetings and that they were not to interfere. He went on to place guards around it and had signs made stating it was an official US headquarter.

It didn't take long for the brass in Shanghi to find out about the place and the place soon became a place for R&R for the brass.

Joe Tully, another communications vet sent me a couple of tales. Now I don't know if this took place while he was at radio school or later, but it matters not when it happened. At one Base where he was stationed he was lucky (?) enough to be chosen to raise the flag every morning on Base. One cold, dark morning he drug himself out of his warm bunk and did as he was ordered and hurried back under the covers for a bit more shut eye. He had no more then dropped off to dream land when he was rudely drug out from under the warm covers, roughly shaken all the way out of the barracks and lectured all the way out to the flag pole. Looking up at the flag he soon saw why all this was taking place. In the cold and dark morning he had run the flag up the pole UP SIDE DOWN! Now that's a definite no-no unless it was a matter of life or death as that is a distress signal and help should be sent immediately. He does not say how or if he was reprimanded or if he even was, but being drug out of a warm bed and lectured all the way out into the cold morning he no doubt felt that was punishment enough and I'm willing to bet that something like that never happened again.

Tully was sent to England and stationed at Station Victor in a quaint little town of Hurley in Berkshire. A few of the Army and Navy men were returning from the town of Maidenhead where they had been on a pub mission. About five or ten miles from Hurley they were fortunate enough to be picked up by an Air Corps truck that was headed in their direction. They were in the back of the truck with an airplane engine to keep them company. Now the driver was a cowboy who did not know the road, but that didn't deter him from going along at a pretty good clip, considering it was night and he was driving under blackout conditions.

Tully and the others kept telling him to slow down as there were more twists and turns then you would see on any backwoods road. They didn't give a damn about him or his truck, but none of them wanted that plane engine parked in their laps if the driver had to come to a screeching halt. The driver finally missed a turn and ran up the guy wires of a pole along the road. This guy now had a major problem since he couldn't back the truck off the guy wires and he could envision his CO's reaction as to how he managed to climb that pole. One of the fella's, Ken Anderson, always a con artist, (as Tully called him) was assigned to the motor pool said he could get the truck off the wire. He went on about how much he admired the flight jacket that was sitting next to the driver and if he would give him that jacket he would get the truck off the wire. Since time was of essence as the driver was due back at the airfield he agreed to the proposition.

Tully and the rest were only about a mile or two from Station Victor so they walked back to the Base and Ken got a pair of wire cutters from the machine shop and walked back to retrieve his beautiful jacket after getting the truck down and back on the road. There were no questions the next day by the local police and of course no one from Station Vivtor could shed any light on how the wires came to be cut.

If you ever see any pictures from that station you will notice that a number of the Army and Naval enlisted men were wearing an official Air Corps jacket. They weren't all issued those jackets. It was the same jacket, they just took turns wearing as the occasion arose.

J.D. Perkins writes from Evansville, Indiana that he joined the navy in 1943 at the age of 18 because he knew that by enlisting he would have a choice of service. By doing this he knew he would be shipped to Great Lakes, Illoinis for his basic training and the girl he loved would be able to visit him. After completing his basic training and because of his ability to learn Morse code he was sent to electronics school at Miami University in Oxford, Ohio. The ten top men in the class were recommended to the OSS who sent two officers to interview them.

After volunteering for the OSS Perkins was sent to Station Victor at Hurley, England in 1943. In early 1944 Germany began its numerous night bombings of England. Hurley was not a bombing target, but was located near several towns that had wartime factories so they heard and saw the bombers flying over their quarters.

Perkins was quartered in a lovely manor house, which housed both navy officers and enlisted men and they were quartered on the second floor.

One night around nine or ten o"clock the Germans started heavy bombing of a town probably less then a mile from where they were quartered. The old house had access to the attic so Perkins and a buddy decided to to go up there to see all the fireworks, which were quite a display. They figured that from that area they would have a spectacular sight of everything going on. In order to see this sight they climbed to the attic and from there to the outside roof. From there they could see and hear the bombs landing, the searchlights pin-pointing the planes and the gleaming barrage balloons over the town. It must have been a spectacular sight.

Everything went fine until they started sneaking back through the opening to their quarters. Perkin's buddy was taller and heavier then he was so the buddy lowered himself through the hole and placed his feet on the rafters in the attic. Perkins then lowered himself down to the shoulders of his buddy and placed his legs around his neck and shoulders. So far everything was going along fine until his buddy tried to lower Perkins and lost his balance and both went through the ceiling and ended up right in the middle of the Officers sleeping quarters. This became instant chaos. Most of the Officers thought for sure it was a bomb coming through the ceiling and some scrambled out and under their beds. The CO, was sitting at his desk looked up and recognized the fancy black aviator boots that Perkin's buddy always wore. The CO muttered rather disgustedly, "Oh no, not you again!".

The next day found both of the sailors busily plastering the large hole in the ceiling of the officer's quarters along with very red faces. Other punishment was not handed out to them, but the red faces they carred with them plus the comments from fellow sailors was punishment enough. They lost all interest in the fireworks going on around the area.

CHAPTER 5
JEDBURGHS

The Jedburghs were a part of the operational groups and were made up of teams of three, one British or American team leader, one Free French and usually one American radio operator. All of them were cross-trained and as Bill Thompson said he did occasional demolition work. Many times SOE or OSS agents were dropped with the group. In the beginning the British were doing this alone, but the Americans soon became a part of this action. In the beginning this group were dropped from Lysanders, but after the Americans entered the war the formation of the OSS American B-24s dropped many groups.

Unfortunately only one Jedburgh responded to my query so I am most grateful that Thompson sent the following story. Thompson was first dropped into France and later was shipped to Kunming, China; today he lives in Leavenworth, Kansas and sent me a tape of a speech he gave before the "Old Bastards Club" at Fort Leavenworth comprised of active and retired military.

Thompson was at Camp Carter when an OSS officer interviewed him and when accepted he was sent to a camp outside of Washington, DC, This camp was at the Congressional Country Club. When he took a cab from DC out to the camp the cab driver commented on him being another spy. From that we can see even at that early date secrets were not well kept in Washington.

As one part of his training the men were taken to a room filled with men in German uniforms seated around the table and the object was that they were to decide which one to shoot first. The one who did not jump up was the one they were to shoot as the ones who jumped up and ran were not as dangerous as the man still sitting at the table-he could have a gun under the table ot some sort of signaling device.

During the entire training they had to speak French at the mess hall or they wouldn't get the food they were asking for.

After the training was finished he was shipped to London and from there to Henley on the Thames to Homewood Hall and parachute training. He went to to say they were then dropped into France and picked up by the Free French and while they were in France they wore green berets. He also said they had one person with them that got cold feet and just sat on the edge of the Joe Hole. The dispatcher then gave that individual a little help by gently giving him a push with his foot and shoved him gently off the edge and out of the plane. I've had this same story from several Carpetbaggers and my husband, Jack, told me that a few times they had to return to Base with a reluctant individual who refused to jump. With this we go to the Carpetbaggers.

Bob Boone at the 22Apr45 dedication of the monument to the Ambrose crew. B24D 42-40997

Bob Boone and Paul Riviere with dignitaries at the St. Cyr-de-Valorges dedication 22Apr45 to the Ambrose crew.

Jack Ringlesbach in his Kilts

Carpetbagger monument at Harrington Air Base

Black B-24 used by carpetbaggers to drop supplies and agents to the underground in occupied countries

Pub outside of Tempsford Air Base
Photo T.O. Rafferty

Temsford Airfield in 1944
June 1944 where M. Fenster and crew took off on the Violette
Szabo mission to France. Photo by Carl Bartram

Runway today following Base at Tempsfort Air Base
Photo T.O. Rafferty

Violette Szabo SOE agent Jack dropped into France.
This is in the old barn at Temsford.
Photo by Carl Bartram

CHAPTER 6
THE CARPETBAGGERS

The Carpetbaggers were the vital air arm of the OSS and I like to think of them as a sort of taxi service for the rest of the OSS as they dropped needed supplies, equipment, couriers, agents and small groups of ground troops (the OGs) to aid the underground in France, Belgium, Holland and Norway.

The British had been doing this for some time and asked President Roosevelt for help. The SOE, the British Intelligence and similar to the OSS, along with the RAF trained the early Carpetbaggers in low-level flying-really at tree top level. I've heard that some in England called the Carpetbaggers the "tree trimmers". While this was taking place their planes were being modified. The inside of the planes were nearly gutted, leaving only the absolutely necessary equipment in them. The outsides were painted black so they could not be seen at night as in the very beginning they flew only when the moon was full. As the war went on this was changed and they flew every night whether the moon was full or not. The ball turret was removed and it was through that hole, called the Joe hole, that the canisters containing the requested equipment and supplies as well as agents were dropped.

The question arises as to how this air arm received the name of Carpetbaggers. There have been several suggestions made running the gamut from the Civil War to the one Colonel Robert Boone, a squadron leader, gave me. It seems that one day General Bill "wild Bill" as he was known-Donovan was talking with his good friend, General James Doolittle and asked for suggestions. Well, General Jim told General Bill that he knew a wild man who had a squadron of one of the best-damned crews in the Air Force. They would go anywhere at any time and do anything. They would pack their bags in a second and be off just like a bunch of carpetbaggers and that is supposedly how the term Carpetbaggers was attached to the air wing of the OSS.

Some may wonder why I saved this branch of the OSS for last. It's really quite simple. I had Jack right here and could pick his brain any time I wanted and he always had a tale. Besides I didn't want any of the readers to feel I was partial to any branch of the OSS.

In October of 1943, Colonel Clifford Heflin, Major Robert Fish and several others attended a meeting in Hertfordshire according to Ben Parnell in his book, "Carpetbaggers" a most interesting and factual book on this topic. At this meeting Heflin and fellow officers met with others from the 8th Air Force thus forming the Carpetbaggers. These men began training with the RAF and SOE at Tempsford, England. These early Carpetbaggers were from the Anti-submarine squadron and the end of November 1943 Heflin was named commander of the group.

When Jack and his crew left Colorado they flew to Stoke on Trent, England and slated to be used as replacements with crews who had lost certain crewmembers. Shortly after landing his pilot, Mike Fenster, along with other newly arrived pilots were called to a meeting at which this new organization was introduced to them. They were told about the OSS and Carpetbaggers and were told that if they and their crew would like to stay together then they should all volunteer for this group. If any pilot was uncomfortable with this they were free to walk out of the meeting and they would then be used as originally planned. No one of these young men wanted to be considered "chicken" so no one walked out. Before the men were dismissed they were told that if they or any of their crews talked about this group with which they were involved with or mentioned anything that they did that person would be immediately taken out and shot. This statement was enough to keep any one from talking about the OSS and the Carpetbaggers for fifty -plus years and even today will not talk to very many people about their years in this organization.

Fenster went back and discussed this with his crew and told them if they agreed unanimously to join this group they could stay together as a crew or they would be used as replacements as they were scheduled. By this time the crew had bonded and wanted to stay together, but there was one problem. The crews for this project was to be made up of eight men and since their crew consisted of ten men two of them had to be dropped. Fenster being a gambler at heart suggested they cut cards to see who would leave. The radio operator and engineer were not included in the drawing and the two who lost out were transferred to replacement groups.

Later when the new crews were called together they were told the same thing as Joe LaMarre had told me once that if anyone ever talked about this organization and what they did they would be immediately taken out and shot. These crews were then sent to Tempsford and began training with the SOE and the RAF. In March of 1944 the English gave the Base at Harrington to the Americans to use as a home Base for the Carpetbaggers.

One of the first things the men did after they were stationed at a Base was to go out and buy a bicycle. This was a means of transportation for the fellas not only on the Base, but also into town or to be used on "pub missions" in the local village.

When Jack asked one of the Englishman on Base where to buy one he was told to go into the village and to a barbershop and he felt sure one could be purchased there. Now why used bicycles could be purchased there I have no idea and today neither does Jack, but he followed the advice of this person and soon came riding back on Base with his prized possession-a bicycle! He used it the entire time he was there and doesn't remember what he did with it when he left to come back to the States-says he probably gave it to some one who needed it.

The bicycles were not only a thing of pride and a source of transportation, but they were also the cause of accidents. The reason for this was most often the difference in the mechanism between English made bicycles and the ones the boys were used to using back home. The American bikes had brakes on the foot pedals where as the English had them on the handlebars and as a result many of the GI's took air-borne trips over the handlebars. When you listen to the many stories about these tools of transportation it seems that each one is different, depending on how much the individual had imbibed at the pub.

There were also other causes for these flying trips some of the men took such as rain or debris on the road with the same results... landing usually in the ditch. Rain many times caused the men to take cover in the hayfields along the road with the sheep, thus providing warmth for the men as they slept off the effects of the night at the pub. This was also the cause of the men arriving late at the Base and required a visit to their CO. The first time I met Colonel St. Clair at a reunion he fold me that Jack had spent so much time in "that chair" that there should have been a plaque with his name on it.

I think the funniest bicycle story I heard came from Jack. He said one night he and his buddies left the pub after a lovely evening of lubricating their livers and he received a ticket for going to fast. He said he was riding happily along and minding his own business when he heard someone flying past him. This person stopped and flagged him down. There stood a British Bobbie and the way he stood Jack knew this guy meant business. The Bobbie lectured him for a few minutes on bicycle safety and followed this with a ticket for riding to fast and told him to take the ticket to his commanding officer. So once again he found himself in that "special" chair in the "Saint's" office.

There were other causes for these flying trips some of the men took, such as rain or debris in the road with the same results.... Landing in the ditch. The rain many times caused the men to take shelter in the hay mounds in the fields along the road with the sheep providing warmth for the men they as slept off the effects of the evening in the pub and often times returned to Base late the next morning requiring a visit to St. Clairs office and spending some time in "that chair".

Colonial Fish tells this story in his book, "They Flew By Night"and has given me permission to use some of the tales he tells. He tells that one night he was about two miles from Base returning from the pub when he hit some debris in the road and like he says, " Thar he flew". He landed in a hedge along the side of the road and fell smack dab in the middle of thorns. He very painfully pulled himself out, got back on his bike and rode the rest of the way back to Base, going straight to the hospital to see Dr. Gans. "Ol' Doc" was not very sympathetic as he had seen many men in that shape before. He gave Fish a shot of bourbon, followed by another and began to pull out the thorns. Even with two shots of bourbon it was still a painful ordeal.

A few days later the order came out that personnel reporting to the Base Hospital with injuries resulting from bicycle accidents while returning from the pub would be subject to disciplinary action. This did not slow down the visits to the pub or bicycle accidents, but now the men nursed their aches and pain in silence. I have often wondered what happened to all the bicycles after the war ended and the men started coming back to the States. This extraction from a 1989 Carpetbaqgger newsletter by John J Kiley and included in Fish's book states that Kiley had sent two forty foot long flat bed trucks to Cheltonham with those bicycles on board per instructions from higher quarters. What happened after that? I'm sure they were put to good use as transportation at that time through out England was still at a premium.

Shortly after a few trips to the pub Jack realized they were being followed....by whom he had no idea. One night Jack, being the top NCO in his crew, was told to gather up the rest of the crew and head back to Base. It seems some one was talking about things better left unsaid. Fifty plus years later he found out that the SOE/OSS were following the men whenever they left Base.

Sebastain Corriere told me the following tale. He said that the flight crews received flight pay, but the ground crews didn't so they couldn't afford to buy bicycles and they had to wait for rides to the pubs, as it was quite a far piece to walk. From time to time the Base would provide a truck to take them into town. The truck would naturally be jam packed with the men practically sitting on top of each other. One night returning to Base a GI sitting near the cab of the truck yelled out that he was sick and going to "puke". Corriere said he didn't know where all the space came from, but a walkway opened so the guy could walk to the tailgate.

Another tale he tells is that when they were stationed at Watton they knew if they were going into town it was a "two boot" walk. One pair to wear from the Base out to the muddy road and carrying the other pair. Upon reaching the road they changed to the clean boots to wear the rest of the way to town and hiding the muddy ones. Coming home however, presented a small problem.... Trying to find where you had hidden your boots to wear on the return trip to the Base. If one was loaded it meant going back the next day and hunting for them.

Again Corriere tells how he was smitten by an English WAAF and they had decided to marry and both had to have the permission of their commanding officer. Corriere took his papers to St. Clair and asked him to sign them and when he was ready to use them he would. St. Clair pointed his finger at him and said, " Corriere, if I sign them "YOU ARE GOING TO USE THEM!"!. End of story. He did go on to say that after returning to the States he married another girl and many years later when they went to England for a Carpetbagger Reunion he and his wife found the former WAAF and they spent a couple of hours visiting her.

My husband tells another similar story. He had met a young lady from Scotland and would go up between missions to visit she and her family whenever he could. He would usually take coffee or some other hard to get items with him that they could exchange on the black market. He would take a bottle of scotch or some other gift to the cook at the mess hall in exchange for these items.

He enjoyed the family life and began to feel very much at home until one time he went for a visit and upon meeting the young lady at her home was informed that her father had made arrangements for them to go to a nearby loch (lake) for a few days. The thought instantly went through his mind that here was a father looking for an American son-in-law and hurridly came up with some excuse for returning to Base. He wasn't ready for that state of marriage just yet.

One of the first things Jack told me was that shortly after their arrival at Tempsford and talking with some "old timers", who had probably been there a week or two longer then they had was how to get to London. He was told that he could take a train to London and once there if they needed help or information they could always talk with a Cabbie.

The next two-day pass that he and his buddy, Dick Thomas, had they headed for London. When they arrived they went to an NCO club they had been told about called the Nut House and Jack immediately joined it, To this day I cannot find any one from the various OSS groups that knows anything about such a place, but it must have existed.

They sat around at the club drinking and talking with others until they realized the day was gone and they had to find a place to spend the night. One of the two remembered the advice some one had given him regarding the help a Cabbie might be able to give them.

They left the club and flagged down a cab and told the Cabbie their problem.

The Cabbie became very friendly and talkative as soon as he realized that the two of them were well on their way to oblivion. Jack later said that after driving them around for what seemed like hours they were finally came to a small place resembling what today we call a Bread and Breakfast. As they were getting out of the cab they asked the driver where they could get a bottle of Scotch. By this time the Cabbie KNEW he had a couple of greenhorns.

They found their room nice, clean and with two beds and they thought they had died and gone to heaven. They took off their uniforms and before they could even open the bottle of scotch they were both asleep. The next morning, waking up, they both found themselves hung over clear down to their knees and maybe even beyond. No need to worry though as they still had the bottle of scotch-a little bit of the dog that bit them would surely take care of that. Thomas opened the bottle took a big swig which he immediately spewed across the room-it wasn't scotch at all. It was COLD UNSWEETEND TEA!

Going back to Base they suffered the ill effects of the hangover and decided it best to keep it to themselves. They later admitted the episode to their better halves and admitted it was a lesson hard learned.

Talking about hangovers here is one that Don Fairbanks sent about a radio operator. All crewmembers thought that radio operators marched to a different drummer then the rest of the crew and since Jack had been one I can verify that. Anyway, after a night of heavy partying in London, Fairbanks and his party returned to their rooms at the Red Cross. A short time later they heard a strange noise coming from the bathroom. When they investigated they found good o'l Fogy, their radio operator, sitting on the floor with his legs around the toilet and his head in the bowl and sending messages in Morse code to himself. The dit-dah-dit came back to the men as a strange echoing sound The rest of them not knowing Morse code wondered if he was hearing a song and trying to send it to a girlfriend or just who was on the receiving end of the message. The next morn after Fogey had sobered up he denied everything. Strange Americans some of the English no doubt thought.

Some of the tales of the buzz bombs the Germans sent over Londoon have left different memories not only for the English, but also the American GIs. Jack tells one night shortly after their arrival at Tempsford he and a couple of crewmates went to London. They were walking along the blacked out streets not having any idea where they were going and they kept bumping into light posts and other things they could not see. Suddenly the bomb alert siren went off and people passed them running to the bomb shelter. Jack, being as curious as one of Dr. Seuisse's cat stayed above ground with a buddy to see what would happen next. They could see the bomb amd hear the bomb coming over and stood there watching when it hit the ground a ways up the street. They heard the air wardens standing outside the bomb shelter say, "Look at those damn Yanks standing there watching that bomb come over." The next thing Jack knew he was lying on ground and had apparently been lying there for a short period of time from the repercussions of the falling bomb. He found the first pub he could and swore that was his last trip to London and began going to Scotland instead.

Colonel Boone wrote that on one of his trips to London with Colonels Fish and Heflin and looking for a fun weekend had taken a room at the Savoy. That night a buzz bomb came over London and blew the window in with the glass falling all over the Heflin's bed. After that he and his friends weren't all that anxious to spend time in London.

A friend of ours, who now lives in Canada, was a nine-year-old boy, living with his family in London during the war. He and his eight year old sister, Pat, shared a bedroom. One night while asleep one of the bombs landed in a nearly street. The blast caused all the glass from the windows to be blown in and clear across the room to the end of the room where the door was located. The effect of the bomb was so great that the wooden shutters that were closed over the windows and held in place by iron bars, in order to protect occupants from flying glass, were blasted off the walls and ended up on their beds. There was so much debris at that end of the room where the door was that his parents could not initially open the door. He does not recall being injured, but does recall all the noise and confusion and fear until his parents could get them out of the room. His sister recalls leaving their beds and following instructions from their father and walking very carefully over a floor littered with glass and finally squeezing out of a partially open door.

After that they were sent to live in a village in Bedfordshire, not far from Tempsford where they had an uncle. John Alcock was a member of the SOE and was engaged in work similar to the Carpetbaggers and later was killed while on a mission.

Bestow Rudolph sent this one to me about one of his trips to London with a friend, a Captain Smith, and they were going to stay at a place about a block past "that big old house where the King and Queen lived" as he put it. At the last minute Smith couldn't go with Rudolph, but told him he would be on the next train. When Smith did not arrive he took the round (?) bedroom so when Smith came he would have the one closest to the door. Seems they always worked it this way so that the last one in would not disturb the first one in. The V-1s were coming over so that sleep was not very sound. Around 7AM a V-1 slipped through the alert screen and landed on the 2nd building from his window. Then as he said, "there was one hell of an explosion". Rudolph opened his eyes and saw the side of his bedroom coming his way. All he could do was to pull the covers over his head and curl up in the bed. When it was over he found he was unhurt except for a small cut on his forhead.

When things calmed down he got up and started to dress and looking around he knew he wouldn't be staying in that room that night. Then he thought of Smith in the next room and made his way to the room. Smith wasn't there! Instead there was an 8x8 bean lying across the bed where Smith would have been sleeping. If he had been in that bed he would have had a broken back. The Captain came in later and they were given another room in which to stay.

That night, even though they were in another room Rudolph frequently didn't sleep to well as Smith said he was up several times that night looking out the window, but Rudolph says he doesn't remember it.

After getting back to Harrington Rudolph went to Colonel Heflin and told him about his experience and thought he deserved a purple heart-the Colonel nearly threw him out of the office.

Some people have problems with authority and respect issues... especally if they think they are not receiving all that they think they should be receiving. I'm not sure if this really happened, but Jack swears it did and from all that I've heard about Colonel St. Clair I believe it could.

When the Carpetbaggers moved to their permanent home at Harrington in early 1944 the entire outfit was placed ono a small hill and lived in Nissan huts. The later crews were placed in tents at the base of the hill. There must have been some animosity on the part of those in Tent City towards those up on the hill.

Anyway the story goes that one fine day a Lieutenant from below came up the hill to place a complaint with Colonel St. Clair regarding some of his NCOs not saluting this Lieutenant when he met them on Base. Now St. Clair was like a "Daddy" to his men and he took good care of them. The Saint-as all his men called him-is supposed to have replied, "Hell, why should they salute you? They don't even salute me! So why don't you go back down the hill where you are supposed to be and don't come back up here!" Now you can see why the men under his command thought so highly of him and respected him.

Which brings to mind another story from Bob Fish's book on this subject. It seems that a Brigadier General called Fish and asked why he didn't teach the 492nd airmen military courtsey and proceeded to tell him what had happened. He wanted Fish to reduce this Master Sergeant to Staff Sergeant. He had no choice except to comply and started his own investigation. When he learned the facts he felt this was miscarriage of justice and did not appreciate the General interfering with his responsibilities and after learning the true facts they bore out his feelings that was certainly a miscarriage of justice.

The sergeant was assisting in the changing of an aircraft engine a B-24 when the General, sitting in the back seat of his big Lincoln drove by. The sergeant was intent on his task and did not think about about a passing General and kept right on working. The General obviously had the idea that when he drove by everyone was to stop what ever they were doing, come to attention and salute him. The General had the authority to demote the sergeant, but Fish being a group commander had the authority to promote him and after ten days he restored the sergeant to his full rank.

After about a month the General called Fish and said he hoped the Sergeant had learned his lesson and that he would have no objections if Fish restored the airman to his former rank...if Fish thought he merited it.

Colonel Fish never told the General that he had taken this very step about a month before the General called. Isn't it strange how even in a war a person's status can be so important to an individual? The King and Queen of England are a good example of this as they very graciously accepted their status.

For some reason, we Americans are very taken with Royalty and the upper class in England. This perhaps was not true in the 18th and early 19th century, but from WW II our attitude towards the "Royals" has changed. Much of this is probably the result of King George VI and his Queen Elizabeth, who left the Americans with a feeling of appreciation for what they were doing for England. They were always most gracious and made the GI's feel most welcome.

Every time Jack saw the Queen Mum on TV he would comment, "She was such a nice and wonderful person". One day I finally got him to tell me why he felt this way. He had just returned from a night flight dropping supplies over France, had been debriefed and given his ounce of scotch, which was given to the crews to enable them to sleep that day and be ready for another flight that night. He was on his way to the mess hall at Alconbury when he noticed a group of officers lined up and standing at attention. In front of this line there appeared several officers and a woman. Being of a very curious nature he lagged behind the rest of the crew and started to amble over towards the group to see what was going on. As he neared the group guards started to wave him off. The lady however beckoned to him and the guards allowing him to approach her. He still had no idea who she was until she very graciously greeted him and shook hands with him. She then asked him where he lived in the States and what his duties were in the Air Force. He answered her questions and realized then to whom he was speaking. After a short conversation he continued on his way to the mess hall, had breakfast and finally to his hut and to bed.

I'm not a very technically minded person and a friend who flies his own plane spent most of one afternoon trying to make me understand the basics of flying a plane. To this day I do not understand one thing about longitude and latitude so flying remains a mystery to me. I often wondered how the pilots kept from getting lost. One day Jack spent a good part of a day trying to tell me, but never quite made it to first base and I still don't understand the mechanics of flying.

In Fish's book, Joe Sowder tells this tale. They took off one night with a load of Germany currency (he doesn't say if the money was bogus or not) to be delivered to the Belgium Freedon Fighters. Outside of Brussels they couldn't find the target or the underground resistance fighters. After circling four or five times they finally located them and made the drop and headed for home only to find they were lost. They flew south towards Paris and over a Nazi airfield where their searchlights found them and he goes on to say,"they shot the hell out of us."

Flying from that field they found they were lost again. All they knew was that they were east of Paris, but just where they had no idea and the maps were of no use. The radio operator finally got a "fix" on their position and they headed home.

The homing pigeon they had dropped with the money made it back to England before they did.

Jack tells about the time they were lost coming back from a drop and headed towards the coast when they hit a bunch of ack-ack and found the gas line to one engine had been hit. They ducked out of the area and headed towards Paris. They were in what they thought was the general vicinity of Paris when the engineer yelled to the Pilot they were headed straight for the Eiffel Tower. Fenster turned away from the Tower and by that time they were really lost. Jack radioed London to get a "fix" and while waiting for an answer they flew over a German field. Fenster turned on his landing lights and headed out of the area. Finally England sent them their location and they headed towards home...so they thought. They always flew across the Channel and this time they found they were flying up the Channel and were picked up by two Spitfires, told to be quiet and to follow them. They were taken to an English Base where they were kept on their plane, under guard and not allowed to leave the plane. Since the crew did not wear dog-tags or had any other identification the English were not sure if they were Americans or not until their identification came thru when the crews did not carry any identification in case they were shot down because if they were shot down by the Germans could take that information and contact Officals in England asking them to contact the men or even to contact their families in the States for more information regarding the crews, their Base andso forth.

Many of the young Germans at that time spoke English as good as the Americans as a fairly good number of them had attended school in America.

Identification finally came thru and the crew was allowed to fly home. By the time they got back to Base they found their mattress all rolled up and their personal belongings together on their cot as they were considered missing in action. Jack said he got more pieces of clothing back then he had before the flight and to this day he says he would love to see the Eiffel Tower in daylight.

Another night the crew got off course and ended up in Switzerland. Coming up out of a valley they found a German plane headed for them. There was a full moon shining behind the German plane so Fenster had a good view of what was taking place. The German plane dropped down and Fenster went up and both planes went on their way. I imagine another pub mission took place after they returned to Base.

All from that era remember the V-mail letters we used to get from our sweeties. The little thin envelopes carried a lot of love. I was living in the Nurse's Home at that time and the word went out that the "mails up" we all headed for our boxes. If we saw one of the girls pull a V-mail letter from her box we knew she would disappear for a while and it was best to leave her alone. At that time everyone tried to be as innovative as possible hoping that different types of letters would bring that special person closer. Remember the SWAK on the back of the envelopes and if it came from a girlfriend it had red lipstick imprints on the back of the letter hoping that would remind a soldier/sailor/marine of the girl back home.

I heard one student nurse tell how someone had written her brother a letter on toilet paper so I decided to try that also. One night while on duty things were quiet and thankfully most patients were asleep so I decided to try the toilet paper method. It would be a two-way present, a letter from his girlfriend and at the same time useful. It wasn't the easiest paper to write on, but it was different form the letters received by his tent mates. I later heard the letter was very popular and soon disappeared down the "drain".

Colonel Boone sent me copies of letters he had sent to his wife, Victoria. She had typed all his V-mail letters he had sent home. Copies of these letters provided a snapshot of life away from home and at war. I've picked out snippets from his letters to give the younger generation a view of that period in our history.

In a letter dated September 15, 1943 he writes how he and some others were in their quarters were making soup, but first asked about the food situation at home. Was meat scarce and how about milk, eggs and fresh vegetables, as well as being interested in food prices. He went on to say they had well balanced meals, but not fresh milk, steaks, fruits or vegetables. He then goes back to telling about the soup and how Freddie swiped some onions from someone's patch, another brought a head of cabbage while he scrounged some carrots and salt and pepper from the mess hall.

They broke opened a box of K-rations to get some boullion and then added some tomatoes. He didn't say where they came from. They were all put in a big tin can (the type or where it came from he doesn't say) and let it simmer on the stove they had for heat in their quarters. About 11PM they had a feast using their mess kits to hold the soup. Another sign of American ingenuity.

On October 18th he writes that Freddie came home that day with an iron! Who Freddie is I have no idea, but he mentions him and Matt from time to time. Boone wonders where Freddie finds some of the things he brings home. That evening they all pressed their pants for a trip to London that they had planned and had already made arrangements for passes and transportation for their plammed trip the following Monday.

Jack told me once that he and others would rinse their pants in gasoline and dry them by holding them up in front of the propellers on a plane to dry them and then place them on the springs of their cots, place the mattress over them and sleep on them for several days thus pressing them.

On September 23rd he writes Victoria that he missed writing for two days, as they couldn't mail letters from London. But he would make up for it in this one and he surely did as he finished it at 1:30 AM. He begins by saying that they arrived at Paddington station about 2:30 in the afternoon and went to find rooms which he said was very hard to do, but they finally found rooms at The Hamilton House where Lady Hamilton was supposed to have stayed. The missed lunch so they went to the Savoy for tea and cakes and found the Savoy to be a beautiful place. It was located on the Thames River and surrounded by lovely shrubbery, it was at that time one of the most famous hotels and he wasn't sure how many kings, queens and dukes had stayed there.

After tea they went shopping, but found they needed coupons for nearly everything and of course they didn't have any. After the fruitless tour they went to the Troccodero for dinner and had a marvelous roast beef dinner and then they began to hit the bars. He compared Piccadilly Circus with the Times Square area in New York City. They ended the evening in some fancy restaurant eating a fancy meal and drinking champagne and finally back to their rooms and to bed only to wake up in the morning with hangovers.

Here comes a rundown of what happened to the rest of the group and I quote directly from his letter, " Matt, the crazy man, met a girl who had some nice friends and took him on a tour of the city. He managed to get into a fight, wreck some joint and escaped the Bobbies by a small margin and on his final lap home he managed to fall off a curb and sprain his ankle. The next morning one of them was up and ready for the day, three were still in bed, Rudy was drunk, Archie was down town and one didn't come home for the night. Matt couldn't walk" so Boone said the "the hell with them" and tramped out the door and went to Bond street where he bought himself a beautiful pipe. He then went on to a prearranged place and time to meet the group and they had lunch. After the meal Matt mysteriously disappeared and the rest wanted to drink so he and Baker caught a cab and place sightseeing.

On their tour they took in Buckingham Palace, St. Paul's Cathedral, St. Margaret's Church, the Tower of London and Westminister Abby where they hired a guide to take them through. This guide "sure knew his stuff and rattled off names and dates until we were blue in the face. King Edward the Confessor did most of the building in 1042 and I nearly choked when I thought how long ago that was. He also built the House of Parliament, Westminister Abbey and St. Margaret's. After leaving the Abbey we went by number 10 Downing Street and learned we had missed the Prime Minister by about 20 minutes."

Boone and Baker found Matt again and they decided to go to the theater, so they booked a BOX no less, at the Strand for 6:30 PM. After that they walked the streets for a while and had tea at the Piccadilly where they saw Charlie drunk as a skunk and Rudy was having a wonderful time chasing a blond around. Then they ran into two of Boone's crew and bought them a drink before shoving off for the show, which was Arsenic and Old Lace, which was one Boone, had wanted to see for a long time. Afterwards they had dinner at the Savoy and drank until time to catch the train at 1:30 AM.

He continues and I quote, " I lost my heart to London. It's a combination of New York, Chicago, New Orleans and San Francisco. I've never seen the like; it's so different from the smaller cities I've seen. Very cosmopolitan! Every race is there and you can hear a language from any country you choose. You can have a drink

With any nationality. Can you imagine what it is like in peacetime with out blackouts or curfews? Wouldn't it be wonderful for us to visit for a few days and then take a half hours boat ride across the Channel to France?"

On September 25th Boone again wrote his wife and again I quote, "Got your airmail dated September 3rd and you asked why I didn't give more news. I'm sorry I just can't do that. Although I am my own censor, my letters are subject to spot check. When I affix my signature in that little circle on the V-mail I'm saying that I have not included any information that would be of value to the enemy.

It's a long shot that an enemy agent would see my letter, but if everyone felt that way then every letter would contain valuable information and be easy to obtain. As a safe guard to my squadron and myself my letters will continue to be uninformative in so far as operatins are concerned. The stories (and let me assure you that there are plenty) will have to wait until I see you amd we get the OK to talk about them." In many cases this would not happen until 50 plus years laters.

Boone wrote Victoria on June 5th/6th that some restrictions had been lifted since the invasion and he could tell her about his last trip to France. A crew from St Clair's squadron had crashed near St.Cyr de Valorges. The country in that area is hilly and the crew crashed into a hill. They lost all but three of the crew and these were rescued from the wreckage, hidden and cared for until they were able to travel again. His letter to Victoria follows:

"Hello Sweetheart;

Because some restrictions have been lifted since the invasion I can tell you about my last trip to France. I was called on the phone and asked to be present at a certain hotel, in a specific little French village at nine in the evening on a certain day where an Officer I had worked with before would meet me. The purpose of the trip. I was told, was to be present at a ceremony to be held in honor of one of our crews that been shot down over France some time back and three of the crew survived." (This was the Ambrose crew, George Ambrose, pilot).

He continues, " Of course I was tickled to go. I flew to one of the larger cities and took a train from there to the village. The train was a funny little thing. It consisted of an engine-a diesel pulling two beautiful modernistic and clean cars at the rate of 15 miles per hour. Getting on was a major battle. I went to the RTO (railroad traffic office) to get a ticket. That was the easy part, but a funny little Frenchman didn't want to let me on as he said it was to crowded. I showed him my ticket with the seat reservation, but he said that made no difference, the seats were already full. It seems they sell tickets on the side and make a little extra money. I ranted and raved and finally swore and pushed him aside, yanked a Frenchman out of my seat, gave him a pack of cigarettes and sat myself down.

Now I'll never forgive myself for not remembering my French very well because every one on the train wanted to talk. I could only get half of what they said and could only tell them a quarter of what I wanted to. It's certainly a novelty to go off into another country on one of their trains.

The ride itself was beautiful, in hilly country. It lasted for an hour and a half. They weren't going to stop at my village and I was going to pull the emergency cord, but we all had become such good friends (the engineer even came back for a chat) that they stopped.

I asked directions at the station and started wending my way to the hotel in this funny little town. I met my old friend halfway from the hotel and we stopped into a small 'hole in the wall' bar for a drink and then went up to our rooms to freshen up and have dinner. We spent three hours eating and talking about the ceremony the next day and about a hundred other things. The wine made me drowsy so I toddled off to bed.

After we had breakfast in the morning we drove to another smaller village where the event was to take place. Here I was taken to the exact place where the plane first hit the ground and eyewitnesses explained the whole thing to me. Then I was taken to the spot where the ship finally came to rest-the place where five of the crew were found.

The French had erected a monument on this spot-a very impressive monument- explaining the reason and naming the five who were killed. I have dozens of pictures of the whole days events that I'll send you when I get back.

After a glimpse of the monument and a talk with those who had seen the crash we descended into the village. Upon entering the town square I noticed there were banners over every street intersection reading, 'Vive L' Amerique' or 'in memory of the five Americans who died here.' and many such phrases.

Each window held American and French flags and streamers adorned every building. I had noticed on the way to the village that there were many people out walking. Now I learned why. They were all on their way to this little village. They came by bicycle, cart, and car and on foot. They came, whole families with lunches and Sunday best clothes on. They came as on a pilgrimage. I could see them winding up through the valleys, converging on our small center. They pressed into the square where we were talking about the day's events.

By now I had met the mayor, the American Council, the American Military Attache', the representative from the American General commanding Southern France, the French Regional Commander of Air Forces and many high ranking French Officals and also lesser titles I had met in previous dealings. I was discovering that this was a truly huge thing of signifiance to the French and of great importance to Franco-American accord. I was surprise at being introduced to a correspondent from the OWI (the office of War Information) who not only represented our government, but the French newspapers and an American controlled French magazine.

It was nearly 9:30 in the morning, so we were taken to the Catholic Church where we had an hour and a half Mass, all of which was devoted to the Americans and the war. I'm getting a translation of the Priest's talk to bring home. I've never gotten up, sat down and kneeled so many times in my life.

After Mass we congregated in the square for a few selections by the bands (there were 2) and saluted to the American, British and French anthems. Then we began the two-mile trek up the hill to the monument. The bands led and were followed by the school children. Now this was something! The village had let the children out of school early for two previous weeks, teaching them to walk in step with the band. It was very impressive!

On the way up the hill people ran ahead to snap pictures-both photo and movies. At the monument the speeches began. I kmew I was going to be asked to speak so I was prepared. I had asked the night before if I should speak in French, suggesting that my friend could write a flowery talk and coach me in delivering it in French, but he said others were of the opinion that it would be best if I spoke in English American (there is a difference you known) and have some one translate. This we did and although it wasn't much or very good, it was what I felt. Here is what I said.

'I have flown 30 missions to France at night. Delivering agents and supplies to the French secret army. I am very pleased to be here on the ground to see the beauty of your country, which I couldn't see at night and to feel the warmth of the people, which I could not feel in a Liberator. I have flown here from an American airfield in England. It is the same airfield where those who were killed were based. I am speaking for them and their families and for all Americans in our group in England. I am touched and moved by what I see here. To me it symbolizes the American airmen lost while fighting with France. I shall take it upon myself to write the families of those who died here and tell them of the great honor which you have bestowed upon them. May God bless you'.

It was translated after every one or two sentences. Through out the speeches I would notice a lady whispering to her little daughter or son and point to me. The little one would then scamper up, push a bunch of flowers in my hand, courtsey if it was a girl, and run back. I was loaded down. Others put flowers on the monument as I finally did with those I had received.

When the ceremony was over we walked back to the village for wine at the mayor's house and lunch (dinner really) in the banquet hall at the best (probably only) restaruant in town. It started at one and at six we were still eating. What a meal! And more speeches from everyone. The wine was good and a full or filling belly put all in a good mood so speeches were punctuated with wit. I was even funny myself although I don't remember what I said.

We had a course of spinach, another of potatoes, then cold meats, soup, roast chicken, veal followed by salad, cheese and then pudding. Bottles and bottles of wine kept coming. Phew, but was I full. Everything seasoned with garlic, but so subtly that I threw caution to the wind and stuffed myself.

After it was over there were lots of pictures taken. People kept coming up to me bringing wine as a present. They were tickled that such a high-ranking officer would come to the dedication. A man came up and gave me the dog tags belonging to one of those killed.

Another gave me a boy's crash bracelet. I spoke with a little lady who had hidden two of the crew who were not killed in the crash and contacted the underground who got them safely back to us. She did a brave and dangerous thing. I spoke with a farmer who had sheltered one of the wounded men, but he had been discovered by one of the Germans and had to flee and hide. The boy was taken prisoner. I had planned on getting back to the Base, but it was to late by the time the banquet was finished, and to early to go to bed, so the OWI correspondent and I drank martinis in a cute little bar in the city until awfully late, talking about most anything you can think of. My eye was hurting by then and I couldn't see very well, but the drinks fixed that up.

I did leave the next morning and have been laid up ever since with Iritis, a very painful thing that feels like I have sand in my eye. I'm in the hospital where they are treating me.

Much love,

Bob"

After reading this I've thought about all the letters written that were saved for years only to be tossed out later by the younger generation who simply did not know their history and that by reading or inserting them in books would have brought history alive for them.

Bill Orban writes that he, his co-pilot and navigator were invited by a marine to a gala affair in Dijon, France. This Marine was the one in charge of training the Joes for their jumps for a coming mission.

The Joes were all dressed in their uniforms and there were French cooks to prepare the meals. Now according to Bill it was a first class dinner and greatly appreciated as at that time they were eating from a temporary tent kitchen and that these French chefs could even make spam look good.

Among the Joes was a man in the uniform of a Storm Trooper amd Bill questioned how they could trust him. The answer was simple. They had ways of checking their backgrounds and if they didn't like what they saw they then saw to it his parachute would not function properly during a jump. I've heard this very same tale from other Carpetbaggers so it must be true.

Another story Bill sent also took place in Dijon. It seems one night the three Carpetbaggers along with this very same Marine went on out and about town. They arrived back at the Base and when the guard at the gate hollered halt this Marine is supposed to have said, "Screw him" and drove right on through with out stopping. The guard pulled out his gun and shot once into the air and the driver came to a screeching halt. These guards didn't believe in fooling around and after a good chewing out permitted them to continue on into the Base. I'll bet that was one Marine who didn't try that again.

Bob Boone came through with another one having to do with a flight to France. One night one of the planes from his squadron landed in a cornfield while taking some agents into France. While landing the plane it nosed over and damaged a propeller and engine. The Marquis (French Underground) pushed the plane into a wooded area and camouflaged it with branches. The next night Boone flew a crew of mechanics along with a new engine and propeller over to the men.

It was a rotten and dark night. The Germans were nearby, oh perhaps about 10 miles or so away, but the underground committee was there using flashlights intermittently showing the landing area. The area was one of the worse he had landed in. The woods grew right up to the landing site, which was extremely short to start with.

Boone came in slow and cut the power and sort of dived in (his words). His first attempt was not very good because he couldn't see the ground, but he was determined to finish the mission so had another go at it. This time he said to the crew, "The hell with the Germans" and flicked on his landing lights. The crew didn't blink an eye and they made a nice landing.

The Marquis didn't mind the lights either and they unloaded the plane. They pushed it over near the wooded area, camouflaged it and the mechanics started to work on the damaged plane while two of the Frenchmen took Boone and his crew by back streets into Paris to an old hotel and gave them a feast.

Boone says they made it back to England before dawn, but they all had terrible headaches.

When Jack and his crew first came to Harrington they were told (by whom I never been told) that the bar maids and cabbies could help with any problems that they might run into. Now whether these words of advice came from local people or by "old timers" who had been there a week or two longer then the new comers.

Today we read about high teas held by many of the English and this continued during the war when many other customs had been dropped, but revived later. One night at the pub down the road from Base Jack got into a conversation with an English woman and during the course of the conversation she invited him to attend a high tea at her home. Since the Base was located in what today we would call the "boonies" and since such an invitation was indeed a rarity he readily accepted it. There was a problem however. It wasn't what he should wear as that would be his uniform, but the problem was how he should conduct himself at this affair. His manners were acceptable in the States, but English culture was quite different and this would be a formal function.

He had no idea whom to ask for help, but an English friend on Base told him to ask the barmaid at the local pub. This he did and she provided him with a list of do's and don'ts, which proved most helpful. He was advised not to walk or ride his bike to the manor house even though it was a short distance from the Base, but to take a cab right up to the door. Upon admission to the house he was to give his name and rank to the butler so he could be announced to the lady of the manor. When his hostess greeted him he was to take take her hand, bend over and appear to kiss her hand, but not actually touch his lips to her hand. She would then introduce him to other guests and after that he was to circulate and speak to other guests. In other words he should not stand around and appear to be holding up the walls.

Things went very well, but soon a challenge presented itself. When tea was served he had to sit down with a cup of tea on a saucer balanced on one knee and a small plate of sandwiches on the other. Eating the sandwiches and drinking the tea wasn't a problem, but somehow he managed.

An even bigger problem presented itself about fifty plus years later when Jack and I attended a reunion in Market Harborough, England. I was in our room getting dressed for dinner when I asked Jack to go to the bar and bring me a glass of wine. He was gone a longer time then it should have taken and I was beginning to get concerned when he walked into the room looking as though he had run into the devil himself. He sat down in a chair and began drinking the wine he had brought back for me and told me of his experience in the bar.

As he asked the barmaid for the glass of wine she gave him a long look and finally said, "Don't I know you?" Jack replied, "I don't believe so as I'm from the United States." She continued to eye him and insisted that she knew him and that he used to come to the pub where she worked during the war. "But that was over fifty years ago! You couldn't have been working at the pub." Her answer ? "I was a lot younger at that time." With that he picked up the glass and came scooting back to the room and by the time he finished telling me what had happened he had finished. Drinking my glass of wine. He later made a point of taking me to meet this barmaid.

Pets on Base also made the men feel closer to home and family while holding an animal close.

One of the first things St. Clair said to Jack when they saw each other for the first time in over fifty years was, "You had a little black dog didn't you?" This amazed Jack that after all this time his CO would remember a little insignificant thing as a pet. He did have a little dog while at Harrington that he named "Jingles" which was what the crew called him. The dog would not leave his bed while they were on a mission and as soon as the dog heard his voice when returning to the hut the dog would start barking until some one would let him out and he would run out to greet him. One time when they strayed off course and found themselves on that English Base for two days "Jingles" went wild when they returned. The other crew living at the opposite end of the hut told Jack that "Jingles" refused to leave his cot unless it was absolutely necessary. When Jack left to return to the states some one else took "Jingles" under his wing.

Another incident Fish told in his book was the one about a dog named "Raunchy". This dog belonged to a Carpetbagger who hailed from Harlton, Texas whose name was James Baker. Now "Raunchy" did not consider himself a dog-he thought of himself as just one of the boys. This dog loved beer and each night you could find him at the Officer's Club. The men would place their mugs of beer on the floor while they played cards or were just shooting the beeze. The dog considered this an open invitation to join in the drinking and would go around sniffing the beer in the mugs until he found one that he liked. He was especially fond of dark ale. When he found one that suited his taetes he would start lapping it up until some one caught him and ended his drinking spree.

Each night he followed the same trail home, in a ditch to the living areas, and followed around certain buildings until he reached the one in which he lived. Many nights he was so drunk it was hard for him to hobble and he always had blood shot eyes. Fish ended this tale about "Raunchy" saying he was a better man then some of the others who couldn't find their way home after a pub-crawl.

Then we come to the one about the pigs. This also came from Bob Fish's book.

Who ever heard of pigs as pets on an Army Air Base! But stranger things have been known to happen. As to the date of the presence of these unusual pets-and I use the word loosely-must have been some time around April of 1945. A Sergeant who had charge of the Orderly Room had two loves, pigs and harassing enlisted men. This sergeant had been raised on a farm thus resulting in his fondness for pigs. He built a pigpen near one of the Nissan huts and fed them scrapes from the mess hall. His object was to raise the pigs and either sell them for profit or to have a barbecue for the men in his squadron.

Later in 1987 some of the men attended a reunion at Harrington and happened to meet the farmer who had sold the pigs to the sergeant and they heard the end of the story. It seems that the sergeant after fattening up the porkers sold them to some other farmer then the one he had purchased them from in the first place. This information of course did not make that farmer happy as he had heardthe sergeant had gotten a good price for them as food was still at a premium at that time. This again showed the ability of the Yanks to make money even in wartime and in another country.

FOOD

Food and drink is one subject men like to talk about, that is when they run out of the subject of girls. Food in wartime England was not always the kind the men liked and they always talked about the good homecooking of the type their mothers cooked. Some of the tales about food are hard to believe, but I have been assured that they are true.

Jack told me about the sausage biscuits he would purchase on his way to to Glasgow, Scotland on short leaves. The train would make frequent short stops along the way to take on or drop off passengers. At many of the stops passengers could buy refreshments. The sausage biscuits always smelled so good that one time he decided to buy one along with a cup of tea. Biting into the biscuits he thought it was different from the ones he had at home. The taste was so odd. Getting back on the train he said something to the railway employee who told him they were made with sausage and sawdust as filler thus cutting down on the amount of meat they had to use and the sawdust held the meat together. He went on to say that after a while he got used to the odd taste and if one is hungry enough anything tastes good.

Can you imagine eating CAT? Another person wrote that he had gone to London and to a restaurant and ordered what he thought sounded pretty good. Time passed and still no food appeared on the table, but it finally arrived and said the food tasted pretty good.

Before he left he asked the waiter what the meat was and why did it take so long to prepare and serve it. Imagine his surprise when he was told he had just eaten cat and that it took so long to serve it was because they had to go out to the alley and catch and cook the cat. He went on to write that it really wasn't all that bad, but it tasted it better before he knew what it was. He also asked to remain anonymous. After a tale like that I can't blame him-I wouldn't want anyone to know my name either.

Carrots today are assumed to be salad material or munching food if one is on a diet or at a party, but back during wartime Carpetbaggers who were a part of a flight crew were served carrots every day. I know carrots are good for the eyes and since they flew at night this food would in increase their night vision-so I'm told. I hate carrots! I was always told as a child that if I ate my carrots they would make my hair curl. Not true. They never did curl my hair and today it is still as straight as it can be with out a permanent. Jack however, loves them so when he cooks carrots I try to eat a few to please him or prepare another veggie for myself.

Another food the crews could not eat were gas-forming foods such as beans or cabbage. I cannot imagine anything worse then to fly for ten hours or more with a bunch of guys who had eaten either of those foods before they took off on a mission.

I promised the person who sent the following tale not to reveal his name and this proves that unbeknown to the cook food in the early stages of spoiling could be served. This friend stated that they lived in tents and the mess hall was the only building on the site during the early preparation of this base. One night chicken-ala-king was served and with in a few hours there were not enough latrines to serve the men, so the men who were able to get out of the tents used the surrounding fields. The next day the fences surrounding the site were decorated with shorts, socks and pants. He went on to say that for the next two days they ate only cheese and crackers.

One fellow on the crew was known to be a wheeler and dealer and would disappear each morning that they hadn't had a flight the night before and wondered where he would go, but he wouldn't tell them. One morning they decided to find out and followed him. He went to one far side of the Base where there was a small farm and entered the house. After a while he left the house and started back to his hut where the rest of the crew awaited him and were full of questions.

Some where and some how he had met the farmer and his wife and was invited to a meal and he told them breakfast would be the best time after nights he didn't have to fly. He also went to the mess hall and received something from the cook that he could take as a gift. He had a bountiful breakfast of fresh eggs and everything that goes with them. After that any time he could weedle something out of the cook he would appear for breakfast.

After listening to him tell about the great breakfasts he had at the farm the rest of the crew naturally wanted to go with him, but he told them that was impossible as the farmer needed the food for his family.

This did not go well with the men and they decided to get even with him and bided their time until one of the fellows received word that he had become a father. Windy, decided the time had arrived and his new baby provided a good reason to celebrate. He went out and bought a fifth of scotch for each of the men (there were four including Windy) and when he gave them scotch he told them that they had to drink the whole bottle and in this way help him celebrate the arrival of his child. After a while the wheeler and dealer passed out before he had finish his fifth and Windy didn't apreciate this. He saw a thermos sitting on the floor by one of the beds and thinking it was coffee pouring it over the face of their crewmate. Well, it wasn't coffee, but was cold chocolate, which didn't disturb their crewmate, and the next morning he awakened to find chocolate in his ears and all over his face and his cot. Windy and the rest of the fellows felt that had gotten even with their crew mate and his breakfast trips came to an end.

Boone and his fellow squadron leader, Rodman St. Clair were sitting around on night complaining of the lack of meat they were receiving in the mess hall and how good a thick juicy steak would taste and dreaming how they might be able to obtain some. Now the knew they could go to their truly wonderful friend-the navy-who was their source of liquor and knew they would help them, but they didn't want to impose their food problem on them. They knew if they passed the hat among the guys they could surely gather enough to buy the meat.

What followed was a scotch inspired discussion and " Saint," suggested they wait until the next day and he would talk it over with his Exec. An Exec. is to a squadron what a secretary is to a small business. Without one the business would simply fall apart. A secretary knows where the bodies are buried. They are the ones who take the ideas and make them work. The Exec really ran the squadron.

The next morning "Saint" went to Sam, his Exec, and told him about the discussion the previous night. Sam thought for a few minutes and said, "So that's the answer". "Saint" naturally wanted to know what Sam was talking about. Sam told him that they had a general fund sitting there with no instructions as to its use. It was obvious it was meant to buy steaks for the squadron!.

Boone and St. Clair knew that must be true and if they took the general fund for one squadron and multiplied it by four there would be enough money for several flights to Scotland and Ireland and each steak feed would be enough money for a party for the entire group. They could bring in girls from the nearby villages for the single men. They would use one of the 2 ½ ton truck to bring them in and take them back to their villages.

Boone never did say how they were able to get flights to Scotland and Ireland or where and how in those countries they were able to get steaks. The parties were a great success and their morale was higher then theirs. See what a little imagination can do? Believe me those GI s had plenty of fun those nights.

These young men were always ready to party. Parties helped to relieve boredom as well as pain. Can you imagine how distressful it must have been to see planes being hit by Germans below and seeing the planes burst into flames? The thoughts going through the minds of the crew made them wonder if that was a US plane and if it was from their Base and were there any buddies in it? As they continued the number of parachutes floating down they knew how many men got out and would the Germans shoot them as they slowly floated down to earth? Were they next in line to be shot down? No wonder they drowned all this out of their minds by drinking when off duty. These men were really boys and had not been exposed to death and tragedy before. As Boone wrote after a week of bad loses he and Fish spent a weekend at the Radcliff Hotel drowning their sorrows and swore that he got the drunkest he had ever been. The hangover that followed was no doubt twice as bad, but he still had the letters to write to the families of the boys who had been shot down and killed in action, taken prisoner or were missing. I don't think any amount of alchol would make it easier.

Boone also sent me a tale of a party that REALLY was a party!. A life long friend and pal of his had been sent to England and he finally found the location of this old school friend. They wanted to get together as it had been some time since they had seen each other. Boone arranged with his friend, Laurence Dickey, to pick him up at White-Church, the airport near Bristol, and bring him to Harrington for a celebration. What a celebration it was! The bar was well stocked; there was plenty of food and even women from the nearby town. After eating, drinking and dancing to the sounds of the big bands, the whistle blew for the women to be transported back to town.

The next morning Boone was ordered to fly a mission of some importance that night so he arranged for one of his pilots to fly his friend back to White-Church. The plane left Harrington and after flying for hours they approached the tower of a Base and the pilot asked for transportation to the nearby town of Blackpool. Imagine the pilot's surprise when the tower told him they could not authorize transportation for a 200-mile trip. The pilot answered back with, "what do you mean 200 miles? This is White-Church isn't it?". The answer they received back was that they were at White-Church, but there 17 towns in England by that name and they certainly were not at the one near Blackpool. Boone goes on to say his friend was a little late reporting for duty after a nearly 200-mile train ride. OOOOH. BUT WHAT A PARTY THAT WAS!

Colonel Bob Boone sent me this story and Colonel Bob Fish had a similar tale in his book. Boone wrote that there were four squadron leaders including Rodman St.Clair, Leonard McManus, Jack Dickerson and of course Boone.

The squardon commanders would meet with a group of officers in the War Room to pick targets for the night from a huge wall map, ome by one in rotation.

After a while this became sort of a game to these officers who were all about 25 years of age and here is how it worked. If St. Clair had first choice he would think " now if I pick this one Boomer (Boone) as second choice will probably take that one, Jack will choose the one over there and Mac will get stuck with the worst."

Now it happened that Mac was the worst poker player and had the worst luck and he most often got the most dangerous targets. Sounds like a bunch of young fellows who felt they were immortal doesn't it?

Many years after their War Room games were over and they were all at a Carpetbagger reunion. Saint had become a very successful businessman and liked to take a large suite and have a dozen or so of them up for drinks before dinner. At this particular hotel his suite had a gigantic bathroom with a huge bathtub that he had filled up to the top and floated gardenias in it and called it his swimming pool. As each guest arrived he would take them in and proudly show off his huge "swimming pool." Some how he had missed Mac's arrival, but finally grabbed him and said, "come see my beautiful swimming pool, Mac." Mac replied, "I already have, Saint and I pissed in it to get back at you and Boomer for all the rotten targets you two guys stuck me with during the war."

Sometimes a naughty work seems to be most appropiate to fit the situation.

To close up this chapter on the Carpetbaggers I have one more to add. I mentioned Joe LaMarre previously, but did want to include this one showing again how the OSS chose it's men. Joe had been employed by the Ford Motor Company at Willow Run, Michigan. LaMarre spoke French, Polish and a bit of German and had worked in the engineering section on B-24s. He was a part time student at the University of Michigan and had a deferment. However many of his friends were going into service and he quit his job planning on enlisting so he could get into the branch he wanted. Before he could do this he was drafted. After his OSS interview he was attending a briefing when General Donovan soon impressed upon them the secrecy of the organization when he told them that if anyone talked about the organization he would immediately be taken out and SHOT! LaMarre said that statement was firmly imprinted in his mind and today still will not say much about the organization.

LaMarre was sent to Alconbury, England where he worked on the modifications necessary to put the B-24s in service. While with the Carpetbaggers he even flew some of the planes he had worked on back home and drew much satisfaction from this and knowing he had done a good job.

Nothing written about WW II would be complete without a word regarding the day of infamy-Pearl Harbor-as President Roosevelt called that day. Now let's hear Colonel Robert Bowker's discription of the events of that day.

A radio blackout was in effect at that time and a warning message was transmitted by alternate commercial channels, but was somehow filed at night letter rate and was delivered by RCA communications in Honolulu by a bicycle messenger for decryption subsequent to noon on that fateful day.

Early that moorning Bowker was awakened by aphone call from the duty sergeant at the Hawaiian Department Signal Office who advised him that war was in progress and he had better report ASAP. Bowker was in communications and after hearing anti-craft detonations and saw black puffs over Pearl Harbor he knew they were under attack. He knew that frequent practices of the anti-aircraft forces were seen as brown puffs so he knew he had better hurry,

His trip to Fort Shafter broke all speed limits, but still had a sad aspect to it as the streets were littered with dead dogs. In Honolulu dogs generally have the right-of-way and would saunter across the streets very deliberately. Many of the dogs were in poor health with arthritis and/or heartworms and traveled rather slowly. This day traffic was not in a waiting mood.

The civil defense forces were alerted and one man with a Springfield 30-06 gave him the choice of either slowing down or getting shot. Bowker knowing the difference between the two choices slowed down. Arriving at the Signal Office he found the Signal Officer working on a draft to the War Department requesting more troops and materiel to convert to wartime status.

He was directed to prepare a similar message of unknown scope or duration. He knew not to question the Signal Officer, as that gentleman had been his ROTC instruction at the University of Michigan. As a result he knew that everything he hoped to be was due to that gentleman. He literally ownd Bowker body and soul, so he took a deep breath and started writing. This went on for about two hours until the Signal Officer decided they should all take a break and have a drink from the cooler, which was outside on the porch.

They had just gotten out the door when there was a terrific BOOM; the tops of several palm trees circling the building disappeared. What ever it was barely missed them and tore a hole in the side of the building, continued on it's way and passed between the arms of the Signal Officer's chair, out the building and disappeared through the side of the Finance Building across the street. Some enterprising GI' s used this convenient entrance to rob the finance office and may still be in Leavenworth. Bowker went on to say that wartime justice was not liberal.

Bowker actually welcomed the Japanese attack in one way as otherwise he would have been required to report to the Base Commander the morning of December 8th. It seems some of his men had complained to the Chaplain that he had worked them all day the previous Sunday and thus caused them to miss church services and, even worse, had worked them through the half-holidays they were supposed to have for exercise. As it happened he forgot to appear for the disciplinary action and apparently the enforcers were VERY busy and it was never mentioned again so Bowker had lucked out.

CHAPTER 7
THE SZABO DROP

When the Carpetbaggers left Harrington on a mission across the Channel and carried agents with them they never knew anything about them and the Americans never used their real names. When Jack received a call from a friend in England this was all about to change.

It was a beautiful summer Sunday afternoon when Jack answered the phone and heard from this friend who was very excited and animated. He had been in London doing some research when he came upon some information on an agent, Violette Szabo. The more he read the more excited he became and hurried to his home in Wellingborough.

One reason he was so excited was because he found this information that he

Had never heard before regarding this agent and the more he read the more excited he became as he felt sure Jack never knew that they had dropped her into France.

Violette Szabo is a much-revered person from WW II and the first woman to receive the George Cross, which was given posthumously to her four year old daughter, Tania. This award is given only for acts of greatest gallantry when all thought of self preservation is subordinated to the call of duty. As King George bent forward to give Tania this medal he said, "This is for your mother. Take good care of it. She was a very brave woman and you must always be very proud of her." Tania's father had been killed in Al Alamein, North Africa and had never seen his daughter.

After the birth of her daughter and the death of her husband Violette was determined to avenge his death and because of her ability to speak fluent French she was accepted in the SOE, which is similar to our OSS. During the war and afterwards many of the young girls in England looked up to her as a model and an inspiration to them.

Jack remembers the afternoon the crew was called to fly to Tempsford to pick up some agents and drop them in France. The crew, as it was routine, did not know the agents they were to drop among which one was an American radio operator. The Carpetbagger crew had been trained by the SOE and the RAF during the end of 1943 and beginning of 1944 so when the British needed a crew to drop these agents and an RAF crew was not available Vera Atkins and the rest of the staff knew about the abilities of the Fenster crew and requested Harrington for their help.

Jack says they never talked much with agents they dropped and never gave them their real names and of course never knew a thing about them. He frequently would tell me there had been one-woman agent who insisted upon kissing every one of the crew members from the pilot on down. He also remembered this young woman as being attractive, but in her jump suit one could not tell much else about the woman. All of the agents wore jump suits and were well padded with money to be used during their mission.

After receiving the information about the drop I mentioned it to one of the Carpetbagger historians who insisted this was not possible, as he could not find a record of the mission. Later after much conversation and American record searching it was found to be true. There has also been some question about the take off site. Atkins wrote that they took off from Tempsford and Jack and the only other remaining member of the crew agree. Here again historians disagree because the mission record for that night does not mention from where they took off.

Szabo and several others about 3 days later were headed to another location when the Germans ambushed them. Szabo had taken a gun with her and with this she held off the Germans long enough to allow the others to escape and she was taken prisoner. She had injured her ankle while learning to jump and this was the reason she was unable to get very far so she stayed behind thus allowing the others to flee.

Szabo was a thorn in the side of the Germans as she defied them at every opportunity until she was executed on January 25,1945. A most interesting book on Szabo is the one written by Susan Ottaway and titled, "The Life That I have".

This woman lit a beacon for freedom, which continues to shine brightly today, and she continues to be a role model to the younger generation in England.

ACKNOWLEDGEMENTS

F irst off I want to state that any errors in any of the tales are mine and not the contributors.

There are so many people to whom I owe a word of thanks that it is hard to know where to start.

To all the people who responded to my query for these stories I owe a big thank you.

To James Ranney for implanting the idea in my mind.

To Colonel Robert Fish for giving me permission to use tales from his book, "They Flew By Night". Thanks Bob for your help.

To Colonel Robert Boone for his enthusiastic support and for his many contributions. With out your help this book might never have seen the light of day.

To John DiBlasi for his support and encouragement when things looked dark.

Finally, but not least, to my husband, Jack, who really got me started on this road called, "writing" as well as for his love and encouragment that carried me through many trying times. He was always there when I needed him most and his meals were always delicious and waiting for me when I quit writing for the day. Without your love and help this book would have just remained a dream Thanks Sweetheart.

About the Author

The author is a native of Ft. Wayne, Indiana, but a Virginia transplant. She graduated from Concordia High School in Ft. Wayne and was a member of the US Cadet Nurse Corps from 1944 to 1947 and received her RN degree from Indianapolis City Hospital in 1947.

She has been writing since high school and everything from essays in high school to patient case studies in nursing to newsletters when she was State President of the Woman's auxiliary to the Kentucky Medical Association. After moving to Williamsburg, Virginia she became an interpreter for Colonial Williamsburg before returning to nursing.

In 1980 she married Jack Ringlesbach and moved to Germany shortly afterwards when the Government transferred him. She returned to her love for writing while over there writing for various newsletters.

She has been published numerous times in the Virginia Gazette, the OSS Communications Vets newsletters, the International Journal of Intelligence and CounterIntelligence and other newsletters.

She has five children, 10 grandchildren and three great grandchildren who moved her to write some children's stories, which remain, unpublished to date.

Printed in the United States
65945LVS00003B/146